The Economics of Henry George

Also by Phillip J. Bryson

The Economics of Centralism and Local Autonomy: Fiscal Decentralization in the Czech and Slovak Republics

The Reluctant Retreat: The Soviet and East German Departure from Central Planning

End of the East German Economy, with Manfred Melzer

Planning Refinements and Combine Formation in East German Economic "Intensification," with Manfred Melzer

The Consumer under Socialist Planning: The East German Case

Scarcity and Control in Socialism: Essays on East European Planning

The Economics of Henry George

History's Rehabilitation of America's Greatest Early Economist

Phillip J. Bryson

palgrave
macmillan

First published in 2011 by
PALGRAVE MACMILLAN®
in the United States—a division of St. Martin's Press LLC,
175 Fifth Avenue, New York, NY 10010.

10 0778 0005

Where this book is distributed in the UK, Europe and the rest of the World,
this is by Palgrave Macmillan, a division of Macmillan Publishers Limited,
registered in England, company number 785998, of Houndmills,
Basingstoke, Hampshire RG21 6XS.

Palgrave Macmillan is the global academic imprint of the above
companies and has companies and representatives throughout the world.

Palgrave® and Macmillan® are registered trademarks in the United
States, the United Kingdom, Europe and other countries.

ISBN: 978–0–230–11585–9

Library of Congress Cataloging-in-Publication Data

Bryson, Phillip J.
    The economics of Henry George : history's rehabilitation of America's
    greatest early economist / Phillip J. Bryson.
        p.   cm.
    ISBN 978–0–230–11585–9 (hardback)
    1. George, Henry, 1839–1897.   2. Economists—United States.
    I. Title.
    HB119.G4B79 2011
    330.092—dc22   2011002890

A catalogue record of the book is available from the British Library.

Design by Integra Software Services

First edition: August 2011

To the memory of my parents,
Ivan Miles and Violet Peterson Bryson

Contents

List of Figures

Preface

A copy of Henry George's *Progress and Poverty* was in my parents' library. It was part of a set of classical books acquired by my mother, who loved to read. It was a remnant from a time when many people read Henry George, although the public of his day was probably not generally more interested in books on economics than the public of today. I didn't actually read the book for another 40 or 50 years, for my interest in and introduction to economics did not happen to be based on George's masterpiece. Still, I ultimately came back to him when an opportunity arose to devote some time to his book.

As an academic, I could not write about George's writings simply to praise them. Any work of economics endowed with inherent worth must be reviewed, analyzed, understood, and appreciated first. Then, if praiseworthy, it should be praised. Since my training and professional trajectory were established long before I came to George, I cannot properly be described as a Georgist, a term and a type that is discussed in the book. Yet I do not hesitate to say that my admiration of the man and of his economics is great indeed. But I wrote the book for another reason. I would like to provide interested readers a single source that addresses Henry George as a person, George's economic analysis, and the nature and impact of his work not only in the era between the Civil and the Great Wars, but also today at the beginning of the twenty-first century.

By searching online, one can find numerous brief descriptions of Henry George's life and the reasons for his fame in the late 1800s and early 1900s. To find a more detailed and historically valuable biography of him, one must turn to the work of his son, Henry George Jr. That book is long and detailed, so that important information about George's life, essential to gain an appreciation of his economic analysis and policy views, is not readily obtained. This book provides a review of the methodology by which George thought economic analysis should be produced. It also reviews more general aspects of his life and work, and how they were informed by his *Weltanschauung* and formal economic analysis. This is done with the hope that it will assist the reader in coming to understand George himself, his thought, and his policy proposals.

An attempt is then made to explicate the analysis that led to the publication of George's most famous work, *Progress and Poverty*. George presents to the world in this work his theory of economic distribution, which fits neatly into the rubrics of classical economics. As George presented his theory to the world, classical theory was already doing its best to slip quietly into the dustbin of history. Alfred Marshall, several other famous European economists, John Bates Clark, and other American economists were developing or in the process of presenting theories that would move the world from the classical to the neoclassical era of economics. Nevertheless, the world at large was unconcerned about the history of economic analysis and George's theory, presented in a rich and competent English, spread rapidly in several languages among the literate classes of the economically developed countries.

Professional economists were sometimes jealous of George's success, and they were sometimes concerned that he did not clothe his thoughts in more modern economic methodologies. In any case, they seemed uniformly opposed, sometimes vehemently so, to George's explanation of the simultaneous phenomena in contemporary societies of progress and poverty. The book therefore addresses the key elements of George's analysis and the way they fit into the economics of his time, as well as to ours.

A very important part of George's analysis, that dealing with the timelessly relevant and controversial issue of free trade versus protection, remains of special significance today. Since free trade seems often to be of interest only to professional economists, the public discussion having largely been given over in the last few years in the United States as a sacrificial lamb to the domain of populist politics, it is of great worth to review George's clear and persuasive arguments for free trade from the perspective of our time. This book undertakes that review.

It will likewise prove to be of great interest to examine George's treatment of the economic resource of land and the national land policies of his time, as well as the significance of his work for the issues of land, urban economics, and urban development in our time. It is in this area that George's influence is apparently the most direct and durable. His legacy in this area is significant not only in academic terms, but also in terms of the policies that are guiding efforts made to rationalize these national concerns both in the United States and in numerous other countries around the world.

The timeliness of George's analysis in the area of land and land policy brings us quite naturally to the final topic of the book. It is implicitly a tribute to George to review the influence that he has had on the profession of economics as a whole. Our discussion will conclude, therefore, with a review of the influence Henry George has had on economic analysis and policy developments in our time.

I am deeply grateful to the Marriott School of Brigham Young University for its support of this research. The School's Dean, Gary Cornia, has demonstrated interest in and support for the project from its inception several years ago. Cornia had not yet become Dean at that time, but he encouraged me to pursue my interest in Henry George and connected me with the Lincoln Institute for Land Policy in Boston, which provided financial support to get the study launched. The Institute certainly cannot be blamed for any inadequacies in this work, for its support did not extend beyond the inauguration of the project. After a slow start reflecting my involvement in several other projects, this one remained on the back burner for several years. I appreciate both Dean Cornia and the Lincoln Institute for having gotten me started on this research. I also owe gratitude for the collegiality of Mark A. Sullivan at the Schalkenbach Foundation for permission to reprint the Andelson article that appears as the appendix to Chapter 6 and for other important forms of assistance. Dr. Bill Batt also provided many helpful suggestions and insights.

Finally, I am grateful to my parents, especially my mother, for having shown me at a tender age the joy of reading good books. I express gratitude for my own life's companion, Pat, for teaching the same thing to our children and grandchildren while providing support for me over the years in the production of a few scholarly books. I accept without rancor the formidable likelihood that those books have contributed somewhat less joy to their readers.

CHAPTER 1

Henry George's Pursuit of Knowledge: On Methodology and Methods

Introduction

Considering this book's title, it is appropriate to ask: Why might one call Henry George America's greatest early economist? Why is rehabilitation necessary? And, how has rehabilitation been happening? These questions will be addressed and the attempt made to demonstrate that George was indeed the greatest of America's early economists. Unfortunately, Alfred Nobel's dynamite idea of a lucrative prize for scientific contributions didn't begin to affect economics until 1968, so George passed away far too early to have received the prize for economics. Since the Nobel Prize is not given posthumously, we have no conclusive evidence that he was the greatest. The best one can do is to offer inductive evidence of his greatness, presenting facts and anecdotes that seem impressive. For George there are many of these, and we will encounter a good number in the pages that follow.

Throughout this work, the principal endeavor will be to present the theoretical and practical contributions of Henry George to the field of economics. Because Henry George is not widely known, even to the best of contemporarily trained young economists, it will take some space to present theories not currently being taught by the profession. We will ultimately turn, however, to the work's implications, its history, and its impact on the economics of our time.

Why does the title talk about history's rehabilitation of George? Why is rehabilitation necessary? Explaining this is much less of a challenge. Perhaps it was because George was self-taught and never attended a university that academic economists, whose role it is to judge the affairs and personalities of economics, were from the beginning not fond of him. They took delight in excoriating his ideas, ostensibly because they were grounded in the methodology of classical economics, which was gradually becoming obsolete. But one suspects that a modicum of envy also motivated the opprobrium of the academy, since George's most famous book, *Progress and Poverty*, had been much more widely published and was vastly more successful than any of the books his contemporaries had ever written.

So for at least half a century, George was terribly popular with the general public, but rather viciously attacked by academics. It would take time for history to sort out the mess. George was actually very competent and understood classical economics very well, so it was incumbent on history to recognize the value of his work. It ultimately did so and continues to do so.

How, then, is rehabilitation happening? Fortunately, for George, economists track not only the differences in important theories, but also the methodological approach taken to develop those theories. Economists seem to have mellowed somewhat with the passage of time, and it has been over 130 years since George's *magnum opus* appeared. Economists now seem to agree that one should not expect a theoretician's work to be grounded in methodologies not developed during the lifetime of that economist. It is sufficient for good ideas to be based on methodologies contemporary to the contributor.

After the originally poor reception of George's ideas, history gradually began to show greater kindness. Economists no longer felt threatened by George's work, so they were not so upset with his lack of formal training. They actually found many of his ideas useful, and some of the greatest economists of our day have paid high tribute to George by their willingness to understand, embellish, and even apply his ideas. The later chapters of this book are dedicated to the attempt to show how this process continues to take place.

It is appropriate to begin our story with a little on George's life and methodology. Since this was one of the problems with his initial reception by the academy, methodology will occupy our attention in Chapter 1, and the discussion will address his life more generally, along with the impact his experiences and personal observations had on his conceptions of economics, in Chapter 2.

Henry George, as we have seen, was not professionally trained in methodological questions, but was hardly unwilling to address questions of methodology and methods; in fact, he did so in a compelling manner. In his later work *The Science of Political Economy,* George (1898) writes almost exclusively on methodology. The clarity and power of his logic are borne on the wings of his exposition. It is remarkable that he was his own instructor. The amount of formal education he enjoyed would be far too little in our day to qualify him to be a high school dropout. But his writings exude literary charm and reflect a thorough understanding of his culture and times and an undeniable mastery of political economy, which remains even today an obscure subject for so many.

I should like in this chapter to review George's own thoughts, not only on reasoning and acquiring knowledge in general, but also on the more complex process of pursuing scientific discovery. I propose to explore the mental methods he claimed for himself to reach understanding, to arrive at the conviction that the academic economists of his day were misguided, and to discover truth generally. In *The Perplexed Philosopher*,[1] George (1892) paused to write of the power to reason correctly. He expressed his conviction that the skill is "not to be learned in schools," which is a strong statement from one who really hadn't attended any to speak of. How would George know that effective reasoning skills cannot be acquired through classroom education? He implied that he had read the works of recipients of such education who had been unable to reason correctly about political economy, although they possessed advanced degrees on the subject.

He was no less confident that the power to reason did not come with special knowledge. How then? The power comes from taking "care in separating, from caution in combining, from the habit of asking ourselves the meaning of the words we use and making sure of one step before building another on it." Lest we mistakenly become convinced that we can achieve this noble objective merely by mechanically tearing words and phrases apart, he adds a lofty admonition to the analyst. The power to reason results "above all, from loyalty to truth."[2]

The next section of this chapter will review George's views of the more formal, proper methodology of scholarship, his appraisal of the methodology of other economic thinkers of his time, and their use of reasoning, statistics, and mathematics. In the following section (see p. 5) we will turn to a discussion of George's basic methods. Here, the concern will not be with pure methodology on the one hand and his theoretical efforts *per se* on the other. This section will consider, for example, George's evaluations of Adam Smith and the Physiocrats, but will also review his attack on his own contemporaries and discuss why he considered them counterproductive in their efforts to advance the science. These evaluations of George are of particular interest because he was convinced that the political economists he addressed should be discredited largely on the basis of their methods.

Such methods were in contrast, George felt, to those that provided the foundation of his viewpoints of the world.

These methods pointed his analyses in particular directions and formed the basis of *The Science of Political Economy*. George had already offered many glimpses into his views on methods and the philosophical underpinnings of his analytical works, but his *Science* offers a systematic view of his basic instincts and beliefs about the workings of the capitalist economy.

Henry George on the Methodology of Economics

It is a compliment to George that this topic needs to be addressed. Many economists of his time would have insisted that George's methodology was an empty set. He was, after all, a writer who had rejected modern economics and economists, accusing the academy of having misdirected the discipline. His *Progress and Poverty*, while widely read, had in their view offered nothing to the advancement of the discipline. It was galling to the academic establishment that George not only came to independent conclusions, but also inspired discipleship among his readers. People without training read George and found that his view of the world was meaningful to them.

Contemporary economists are less offended by George, who has now slipped into a distant age and time. Further, his theories did not anticipate current analytical penchants in any particularly constraining or challenging way. So, current economists in their pursuit of divergent strands of thought would simply suggest that those who find George's work of interest should develop and refine his ideas. It is widely acknowledged that his perspectives retain strong relevance in contemporary issues such as land use, urban development and planning, taxation, and property rights. Contemporary economists would generally agree that it makes sense to utilize those ideas in a manner that will "extend their range of relevance"[3] in those areas.

George's work has found a certain degree of validation from the discipline's most celebrated historian of economic analysis. Joseph Schumpeter, who found George's phraseology unorthodox, asserted that except for his policy panacea (the single tax), the pioneering American scholar "was a very orthodox economist and extremely conservative as to methods."[4] Schumpeter observed that George's methods were those of the English classics and that his favorite among their number was Adam Smith. He asserted that George simply failed to understand Marshall and Böhm-Bawerk, the leading European lights of George's time. But Schumpeter did not see this as a major problem, since George was "thoroughly at home in scientific economics"[5] through the works of John Stuart Mill, who had ceased to write historic contributions only shortly before George took up his pen. George is credited with not having shared the "current misunderstandings or prejudices concerning Mill's work."[6] Schumpeter concluded his brief evaluation with the following: "Even the panacea—nationalization not of land but of the rent of land by a confiscatory tax—benefited by his competence as an economist, for he was careful to frame his 'remedy' in such a manner as to cause the minimum injury to the efficiency of the private-enterprise economy."[7]

George's Methodological "Calling"

It was George's opinion that methodological problems in the political economy of his age made it necessary for him to become involved. The need for someone to step in and guide the profession to appropriate conceptions arose simply because Adam Smith had defined wealth inadequately. The upshot was increasing confusion as to its proper definition, for wealth is the fundamental concept of the science of political economy for Henry George. He was convinced that in the period after Smith and his French contemporaries, the Physiocrats, things had gone downhill for the discipline, reaching a state of confusion with the professors of George's time.

Induction versus Deduction in George's Works

The order of these two types of reasoning is as George prioritized them, induction being the first or primary approach to an analysis of facts. In his *Science of Political Economy*, deduction was seen as the second or "derivative" method. Induction "must give the facts on which we may proceed to deduction," George instructed.[8] The scholar cannot begin to think deductively about a proposition until the basis of such reasoning is established through inductive processes. If this first step is not undertaken effectively, inductive processes will produce analytical flaws. Through induction properly applied, one can grope for a law of nature. George's "scientific induction" represents the preliminary stages of analysis. Once this has been achieved, we can use deduction to understand a given law of nature better. Both methods are proper in the preliminary stages of scientific induction as an analyst gropes for a law of nature; when a law has been discovered, deduction can be used to enable us to proceed from the general to the particular. That step is direct and far less tedious than the difficult method of induction. To verify the conclusions reached, however, we resort again to the more demanding process of inductive reasoning.

George explains that there is an additional investigative method that consists of a combination of the two already discussed and that is most effective in the physical sciences. When induction suggests there is some natural law and analysts can surmise or suspect what it is, they may tentatively assume its existence and observe whether particulars will fall into place as they proceed to make analytical deductions from that assumed law. George calls this the "method of tentative deduction, or hypothesis."[9]

The Methodology of the "Imaginative Experiment"

Returning to the more common inductive investigation classical economists utilized to establish the relationships they often labeled as "laws," and to the deductive manipulation of those fundamental principles, George declared that the most useful analytical tool is a form of hypothesis, a "mental or imaginative experiment." This is a method that enables us to separate, eliminate, or combine conditions "in our own imaginations, and thus test the working of known principles."[10] To the contemporary scholar who would prefer to use his imagination only to determine a set of likely interactive explanatory variables while culling econometrically through a large database, this sounds like a very homely use of the scholar's imagination. George, insists, however, that this is a "most common method of reasoning, familiar to us all, from our very infancy. It is the great working tool of political economy, and in its use we have only to be careful as to the validity of what we assume as principles."[11]

George provides an illustration of how such reasoning works. Because the passage is relatively brief, and because it provides considerable insight into the way George thought and felt about the mental capacity that should be common to all pursuers of truth, I reproduce it here:[12]

When I was a boy I went down to the wharf with another boy to see the first iron steamship that had ever crossed the ocean to Philadelphia. Now, hearing of an iron steamship seemed to us then a good deal like hearing of a leaden kite or a wooden cooking-stove. But we had not been long aboard of her, before my comrade said in a tone of contemptuous disgust: "Pooh! I see how it is. She's all lined with wood; that's the reason she floats." I could not controvert him for the moment, but I was not satisfied, and sitting down on the wharf when he left me, I set to work trying mental experiments. If it was the wood inside of her that made her float, then the more wood the higher she would float; and, mentally, I loaded her up with wood. But, as I was familiar with the process of making boats out of blocks of wood, I at once saw that, instead of floating higher, she would sink deeper. Then, I mentally took all the wood out of her, as we dug out our wooden boats, and saw that thus lightened she would float higher still. Then, in imagination, I jammed a hole in her, and saw that the water would run in and she would sink, as did our wooden boats when ballasted with leaden keels. And thus I saw, as clearly as though I could have actually made these experiments with the steamer, that it was not the wooden lining that made her float, but her hollowness, or, as I would now phrase it, her displacement of water.

This process of isolating, analyzing, and combining economic principles is something with which George felt all scientific types are familiar. We can extend or diminish the scale of a given proposition, put them under a "mental magnifying-glass," or permit the observed phenomena to be perceived under a larger scope. Each individual has to do this for himself, so George suggests that the reader be prepared to do so; he also expresses his preference that the reader place no trust even in George's own analysis without first subjecting it to this very process.

Contemporary scholars may find such a description of logic somewhat lacking in sophistication as compared with mathematical inference combined with the number-crunching and design power of modern computation. But the scholarly work that provided the foundations of contemporary social science, proceeding from a time even before the publication of the *Wealth of Nations* and extending into the latter half of the 1900s, was based on precisely this methodological approach to understanding. Our current appreciation for the tools of econometrics and the powers of computation should not keep us from admitting that the best of scholarly work today proceeds on the same basis. Perhaps it would have sounded more familiar had George simply made an appeal to careful and consistent thinking and observation of the phenomena we research.

George's optimistic view of the general power of reason did not keep him from realizing its limitations. In the social sciences, multicausality can complicate things immensely, and he recognized an "almost endless multiplicity of causes" operating in society. That rendered the kind of reasoning George had in mind, and which logicians of his day referred to as the "method of simple enumeration,"[13] less than fully adequate for economic analysis. Of course, one can conceptualize the multiple causative effects that we attempt to isolate through partial derivatives and multiple regressions. But one must concede that with the presence of good data, the reflective mind is greatly aided by contemporary quantitative analysis.

George's Suspicion of Statistics

It is apparent that Henry George and his contemporaries could not have foreseen in the nascent statistics of their time the potential of the tools of econometric analysis to support the economist's reasoning power. He had respect for the statistical methods of his day, acknowledging that "figures cannot lie," but pointed out that in collecting and grouping them we must be cautious of the liability to oversight and the temptation the analyst faces to promote his biases through the use of statistical sophistry. They may proffer a compelling "appearance of exactness," but be subject to "the wildest assumptions" and the most serious errors.[14] As a result, statistics should not be trusted in matters of controversy until they have been examined painstakingly.

George calls on Cairnes's pessimistic evaluation of quantitative methods in the political economy of the period to buttress his point. In *The Science of Political Economy* he reproduces the Cairnes complaint that the subject had been "constantly assuming more of a statistical character; results are now appealed to instead of principles; the rules of arithmetic are superseding the canons of inductive reasoning till the true course of investigation has been well-nigh forgotten, and Political Economy seems in danger of realizing the fate of Atlanta."[15]

Of this, George wrote as follows:

> At the present time it is clearly to be seen that the worst fears of Cairnes have been more than realized. The period of controversy instead of having passed, had indeed, it has since been proved, hardly then begun. The accelerating tendency since his time as in the period of which he then spoke, has been away from, not towards, uniformity; controversy has become incoherence, and what he then thought to be the science of political economy has been destroyed at the hands of its own professors.[16]

But George had more than methodological reservation toward the inchoate quantitative bent of the professors. A deeper aversion had already been revealed in *Progress and Poverty* when George wrote of Malthus that he "lays great stress upon his geometrical and arithmetical ratios, and it is also probable that it is to these ratios that Malthus is largely indebted for his fame, as they supplied one of those high-sounding formulas that with many people carry far more weight than the clearest reasoning."[17]

Marshall vs. George on Methodology

Let us now briefly consider the views of Alfred Marshall on methodology. Marshall was a leading light among a number of economists from several countries who were developing a new approach to economic analysis.[18] His use of statistics was much like that of George's, consisting largely of thinking carefully about a modest set of numbers and their implications. Marshall was the standard-bearer for a more "modern" economic analysis, but one that could not yet employ the statistical techniques available in our time. He defended the analytical tools available to him as follows: what appears to be a few "scrappy conceptions," terms like "final utility" and "marginal production," are employed so that nonspecialists can gain the advantages mathematicians enjoy from their training when they analyze economic growth. Experience gained in their use, Marshall believed, enabled teachers of economics to help students benefit greatly from them. He expressed the notion in this way:

> Science, like machinery, must begin with scrappy operations. Analysis is nothing else but breaking up a complex conception into scraps, so that they may be easily handled and thoroughly investigated. Afterwards the scraps have to be put together again, and considered in relation to many other complex notions, and the intricately interwoven facts of life.[19]

Note that Marshall's view was driven by a superb knowledge of the mathematics of his day; he was, after all, educated in that field. But his actual description of the economist's methodology doesn't read much differently from George's. According to Marshall science demands that economists study facts and determine which of them are representative of the norm. They must then consider and analyze normal conditions, at first narrowly; with growing understanding, they should investigate a wider range of normal conditions, so that the analysis becomes increasingly complex and closer to the real world. But for all practical purposes, Marshall believed that analysis alone could never complete the task of understanding. "The finishing touches must always be given by common sense," he wrote, "as the products of even the finest machinery need to be finished off by handicraft."[20] Although Marshall conceded that scientific analyses were sometimes clumsy in their first efforts, he was confident that they were "changing the face of the world: because their progress is cumulative throughout the whole life of the race, while each man's common sense, like his skill in handicraft, dies with him."[21]

Marshall's views on methodology thus seem to be similar to those expressed by George. Although the latter would not have emphasized any potential role for formal (mathematical/statistical) analysis and would likely not have been as impressed with the cumulative progress Marshall cited in the above paragraph, he certainly would have agreed with the stipulated roles for careful reasoning and common sense.

Henry George's Basic Methods and Approach to Economics

Let us now consider George's scholarly methods more broadly. Rather than focus on strictly methodological questions, it is instructive to consider the thrust of his more general theoretical efforts and philosophical viewpoints. Of concern are his *Wirtschaftlicheweltanschauung* or economic perception of the world.

Seeking a Definition of Wealth

George was convinced that understanding and consensus could be achieved on scientific issues only if those issues were clearly and correctly defined. Reasoning that proceeded on the basis of such definitions could be productive of positive scientific achievement. He was further convinced that a basic problem with the political economy of his day was the failure to reason correctly about scientific phenomena related to wealth, precisely because wealth had not been carefully and correctly defined.

In a passage addressing Marshall's treatment of wealth, George burdened Marshall's *Principles* in advance with the compliment of "being the latest and largest, and scholastically the most highly indorsed, economic work yet published in English." Then George writes:

> It cannot be said of him, as of many economic writers, that he does not attempt to say what is meant by wealth, for if one turns to the index he is directed to a whole chapter. But

neither in this chapter nor elsewhere can I find any paragraph, however long, that may be quoted as defining the meaning he attaches to the term wealth. The only approach to it is this: All wealth consists of things that satisfy wants, directly or indirectly. All wealth therefore consists of goods; but not all kind of goods are reckoned as wealth.[22]

As we would expect, George did not limit his research on this issue to Marshall's work, for as a good classical economist he would already have referenced the basic sources before having recourse to the Cambridge professor. He began his search with Adam Smith and the Physiocrats.

George on Adam Smith and the Physiocrats

In a day when many were writing tomes on political economy, the father of that science added his *magnum opus* to a growing collection of them. Rather than *Political Economy,* Smith entitled his work *The Wealth of Nations.* George therefore dutifully declares that "the wealth of nations" is the "proper subject-matter of what is properly called political economy."[23]

But if George expected to find a good definition of wealth in Smith's ponderous *Wealth,* he was to be disappointed. He discovered that Smith had not really defined wealth, or for that matter, its sub-term "capital." Nor had Smith really made clear, George complained, the "division of their joint produce between the human factor and the natural factor, nor venture to show what was the cause and warrant of poverty."[24] But there was more: Smith had actually contributed one of history's greatest books without having left political economy axioms to correlate or, for that matter, to hold the discipline's great conceptions together. In spite of Adam Smith's failure to establish clear principles for the science, George writes with some irony of him: "such was his genius and prudence, and his adaptability to the temper of his time, that he got a hearing where more daring thinkers failed, and a science of political economy began to grow on his foundations."[25]

George was decisive in his insistence that one could not develop a science of the production and distribution of wealth if the aspiring scientists could not decide what they mean by wealth. If they cannot do that, he thought, they will not be able to understand each other or even understand themselves. His specific problem with Adam Smith was that political economy's Founding Father apparently had sometimes inadvertently fallen into the inconsistency of "classing personal qualities and obligations as wealth."[26]

For Henry George, the production of wealth entailed only the items that increase the aggregate of wealth. To destroy certain items would decrease the aggregate of wealth and those items therefore also represent wealth. The key to defining wealth is to understand what these items are and what their nature is. Having fashioned this implicit definition of wealth, George himself wondered why political economy should be limited to the production and distribution of this narrow view of wealth. He asked rhetorically whether the proper object of the science of political economy should not also be concerned with the production and distribution of human satisfactions through material *services* that are not concrete in form. Ultimately, however, he denied any obligation to approach wealth in this manner, since he was not trying to establish a new science with new terms. Rather, he wished merely to ameliorate an old and established science with accustomed terms, questioning or revising such terms only when they obviously led to erroneous conclusions.[27]

Adam Smith began on the right track, in George's view. He was right to contend that "the produce of labor constitutes the natural recompense or wages of labor." But in the age in which Smith wrote, this sentiment, expressed as a theory of wages, was not only lacking in political correctness, it was almost revolutionary. So, according to George, Smith suddenly abandoned this view of wages and adopted the alternative—the capitalist producer provides "from his capital the wages of his workmen." This position unfortunately gave rise to the misconception that political economy was a scientific demonstration "that the shocking contrasts in the material conditions of men which our advancing civilization presents, result not from the injustice and mistakes of human law, but from the immutable law of Nature— the decrees of the All-originating, All-maintaining Spirit."[28] Smith's revised theory of wages, the "iron law of wages," attributed low wages and poverty to this apparent "principle" of political economy. But this approach, like that of Christianity in religion, turned the blame for poverty away from the rich employers back to the poor workers themselves. Smith's perceptions of the natural equality of men ceased at that point to enter into his political economy and it proceeded to become in fact "the dismal science."[29]

As for the Physiocrats, George was willing to credit them with greater consistency. They clearly established the principle that nothing lacking material existence, or that which was not the product of land as traditionally defined by political economists, could be considered a part of society's wealth. Quesnay, the leading figure among these French economists, and his followers called society's fund of wealth the "*produit net.*" This net product was what remained after all the landowner's expenses of production were deducted as compensation for the exertion of individual labor.[30] George noted that the actual meaning of the Physiocrats' "*produit net*" was what was understood in English by the word "rent" when used in the technical, political economy sense it acquired from Ricardo.

Given this view, the Physiocrats characterized agriculture as the only "productive" occupation. Although all others might be ever so useful, they were regarded as sterile, since by assumption none of those occupations gave rise to a net product. They did nothing more than return to the general fund of wealth, or gross product, the equivalent of the already-extant material things taken from the fund to be changed in form, location, or ownership.[31] Thus, the Physiocrats advocated the imposition of an *impot unique*, a single tax upon economic rent or the surplus product. Like George, they advocated that all other taxes on the production, exchange, or possession of wealth in any form be abolished. The public revenues were to be drawn from the net product or from economic rent.

George objected to the Physiocratic conclusion that the unearned increment of wealth or net surplus sprang from rent. Considering agriculture the only productive occupation and the agriculturist the only real producer, the Physiocrats had insisted, absurdly, that manufacturing and commerce added nothing to the sum of wealth above what they took from it. This weakness in the thinking of the Physiocrats and the erroneous terminology that it caused them to adopt (about what was "sterile") ultimately caused even their truths and noble teachings to be discredited. This was the more so inevitable because those principles were unpalatable to the powerful interests that seem always to profit from social injustice. Moreover, the habit of regarding land solely from the agricultural point of view was also responsible for converting what is really a spatial law of all production into "an alleged law of diminishing production in agriculture."[32]

In George's view it was unfortunate that this basically correct theory was unable to make a long-term contribution to the progress of truth. The resistance of powerful special interests was able to bring about the overthrow of Physiocratic principles and prevent the application (or even serious consideration) of the justice and potential effectiveness of their practical proposals.

Economists Must Use Ordinary English

George noticed that when the physical sciences observe that a group of things have a particular set of common categorical qualities, they are considered a class and endowed with a special name. Or, when a new concept emerges, it will be labeled with a new technical term. But economics cannot venture to follow this example. Political economy must accommodate itself to familiar, everyday terms, which should be used as far as possible as they are commonly used.

He faults Immanuel Kant for writing with "ponderous incomprehensibility." Whether this trait was common before Kant or became so because of him, George observes a peculiarly German facility for inventing words that facilitate philosophic juggling. Kant suggested the term "antinomy," which suggests the idea of a conflict of laws and which is employed to mean a self-contradiction or mutual destruction of unavoidable conclusions of the human reason—a what must be thought of, yet cannot be thought of. Thus, the word antinomy in the scholastic philosophy that has followed Kant takes the place of the word mystery in the theological philosophy as covering the idea of a necessary irreconcilability of human reason.[33]

George then reviews how Schopenhauer, a student of Kant, extended the idea of a form of reason that transcends distorted human reasoning. George found this philosophy of negation a form of nineteenth-century Buddhism without the softening features of its Asiatic prototype. Such reasoning, which makes us but rats in an everlasting trap and substitutes for God an icy devil, is the outcome of the impression made upon a powerful and brilliant but morbid mind by "the industrious study of a logomachy made up by monstrous piecings together of words which abolish and contradict one another." It strives to turn human reason as it were inside out and consider in the light of what is dubbed "pure reason" the outside-in of things.[34]

Having established the importance for scholars of refusing to deceive themselves or their readers or students with incomprehensible jargon or to invent terminology designed to obscure rather than to illuminate, he was ready to take on his contemporaries.

The Economics of George's Time: The University Professors

George willingly conceded that the works of his time contributed by professors of political economy, whether entitled *Elements of Economics, Principles of Economics,* or *Manual of Economics,* were treatises on political economy. But a strict categorization of their content would disqualify them as treatises on the *science* of political economy; they were in actual fact treatises on what might better be termed the "science of exchanges, or the science of exchangeable quantities." To George, the distinction was important, since these methods were not those of political economy, but represented a science more akin to the science of mathematics. He likewise found the intent of the professors of political economy to substitute for the term (and the field) "politico-economic" the more fashionable term "economic" most inappropriate. To George, it was simply dishonest to try to pass off their "science of economics" as if it were the science of political economy.[35]

To explain how this transformation could be occurring, George resorted to psychology, expressing the viewpoint that the economists were simply following a herd instinct rather than thinking for themselves. "This is of human nature," he said. "The world is so new to us when we first come into it; we are so compelled at every turn to rely upon what we are told rather than on what we ourselves can discover; what we find to be the common and respected opinion of others has with us such almost irresistible weight, that it becomes possible for a special interest by usurping the teaching province to make to us black seem white and wrong seem right."[36]

An academic discipline may consist, George believed, of a group of indoctrinated individuals devoting considerable time to rationalizing away incongruities in the philosophical system of conventional wisdom. Their abilities are required to accommodate all facets of the theoretical system to any troublesome incongruity. This was often accomplished so successfully that philosophical systems survived what should have been fatal incongruities for generations. This demonstrates, George writes, that "the mind of man is even more plastic than the body of man."[37] The "artificialities and confusions" the professors had to invoke to make incongruities tolerable in these processes of systemic rationalization "cannot be understood except by those who have submitted their minds to a special course of cramping, become to them a seeming evidence of superiority, gratifying a vanity."[38]

George was fully aware what these accusations would cost him. He was making himself a perpetual outcast of the academic establishment, but he felt confident that what he was saying was true; he never looked back and never sought academic honors. He found it amazing that academics could have devoted years of their lives to learn how to pursue truth, only to refuse to give honest consideration to correct principles when they encountered them. Rather than embracing obvious truths, they circled the intellectual wagons to defend the badly misguided academic consensus. George's role, as the outsider, was to attempt to instruct them on the fundamentals of their science, having "never seen the inside of a college," except when trying to teach the professors what they should have already understood. They could clearly never accept as their teacher one "whose education was of the mere common-school branches, whose alma mater had been the forecastle and the printing-office." That such an individual should be permitted to prove their inconsistencies "was not to be thought of."[39]

George and The Austrian School

Schumpeter's assertion that George failed to understand Marshall or the Austrian Böhm-Bawerk has already been noted.[40] Let us consider briefly George's attack on Böhm-Bawerk and those of like mind based largely on their failure to make the classical distinction between value in use and value in exchange. When value was in fact considered by the Austrians, their undistinguished "value" was made an expression of the intensity of desire, so that it was reduced to purely subjective origins. It was simply a matter of psychology. The theory fixes the extreme or marginal utility of a commodity by the "intensity of the desire" of the consumer.[41]

George was unable to perceive the value of the marginal utility theory. He found it an "elaborate piling of confusion on confusion," the inevitable product of a careless use of words. The Austrians, like their American counterparts, failed to make clear definitions before beginning to try to reason from their postulates. Nothing could more strikingly illustrate the problems that arise from poor use of words in political economy than the Austrian value theory.[42]

George himself did have (and faithfully retain) his own, carefully crafted definition of value, which "is equivalent to the saving of exertion or toil." The value of anything, he taught, "is the amount of toil which the possession of that thing will save the possessor, or enable him, to use Adam Smith's phrase, 'to impose upon other people,' through exchange."[43] If individuals wish to determine an object's precise value, they simply submit it to competitive offers, as at an auction. But George does not seem so far from the Austrians when he defines value (in its economic sense of value in exchange) as having no direct relation to any inherent quality of external things, "but only to man's desires." Its subjective, not objective, nature lies "in the mind or will of man, and not . . . in the nature of things external to the human will or mind."[44]

So much for George's conception of value. But what is wealth? Articles of wealth uniformly possess value, the loss of which would cause them no longer to qualify as articles of wealth. On the other hand, all items of value cannot be classified as wealth, which George insisted was erroneously done in the economics texts of his time. As evidence, he refers to the widely used textbook of his rival, Francis A. Walker.[45] George parted ways with contemporaries such as Walker when they classified the production of services or information as wealth. He insisted that producers of services (e.g., barbers, bootblacks, musicians, surgeons, teachers, nurses, poets, or priests) do not technically participate in producing wealth. He granted that it would be misleading to think of them as nonproducers. They are simply not producers of wealth, although their production may be of great worth. They are, after all, producers of utility and satisfaction; moreover, they may provide indirect assistance in the production of wealth itself.[46]

From "Value from Obligation" to the Right to Collect Rent

George's assessment of value was in part historical in approach. The large landholders of feudal times had enjoyed traditional prerogatives that were clearly of value, for example, "the right of holding markets, of keeping dove-cotes, of succeeding in certain instances to the property of tenants; or of grinding grain, of coining money, of collecting floatwood, etc."[47] These were "values from obligation" that have, through the passage of time, merged into the single right of exacting a rent for the use of land. This was, of course, a historical breach of the principle that the land should belong to everyone in common. Over time the land was expropriated by more-or-less random social processes favoring the aristocracy and, later, the landowners. George was perfectly willing to put these "property-rights" relationships into terms of morals and declare the rich to be robbers, since at the very least they share in the proceeds of robbery. It follows that the poor are the robbed, and that was why George exclaimed: "Christ, who was not really a man of such reckless speech as some Christians deem Him to have been, always expressed sympathy with the poor and repugnance of the rich . . . If there can be no poor in the kingdom of heaven, clearly there can be no rich!"[48]

George on Socialism's Fatal Defect

Throughout his writings, George constantly advocates market forces and the market system. Karl Marx, a contemporary of George, was the spokesman of a minority view of the world that was not of great interest to most serious economists. George believed socialism to be burdened with a serious, even fatal, defect.

This is the fatal defect of all forms of socialism: any attempt to carry conscious regulation and direction beyond the narrow sphere of social life in which it is necessary, inevitably works injury, hindering even what it is intended to help.[49]

George held that the full powers of man may be utilized only in independent action. Subordinating one human will to that of another may in certain ways secure unity of action. But doing so where intelligent effort is required must always involve the loss of productive power. This truth is particularly evident in the experience of slavery, but also in other instances where governments follow their universal penchant to pursue actions inimical to the freedom of the individual. George also penned the corollary to the principle: where unified effort can be secured without limiting in any way the individual's freedom, the whole of productive power may be engaged with immeasurably greater results.[50]

Competition: the Motive and Productive Power of Exchange

George uses his definition of value to analyze competition and exchange. The motive of exchange, the primary postulate of political economy, is to enable men to gratify their desires with the least exertion. He sees competition as the "life of trade." But in the literature of his time, he found the quite ubiquitous assumption that competition is an evil that should be restricted or even abolished in the interests of society. It was therefore worthwhile to consider carefully its "cause and office" in the production of wealth.[51]

The assumption that competition had to be evil arose from the widely observed practice of taking unfair advantage of others by distorting the laws of distribution of wealth. This assumption was considered by George to be an apt characterization of the socialism of Adam Smith's time, known as the mercantile system. The system was still extant in George's time, he acknowledged, and its strength had not diminished significantly under its current instrument of protectionism. Many of the associated and misguided views deprecating competition originated from righteous indignation with the extreme inequalities in the "civilized world's" distribution of wealth.

The law of competition, in George's view, was one of those natural laws that required understanding if the associated economic system were to be valued. That intelligence "to which we must refer the origin and existence of the world" foresaw that the progress of civilization "should be an advance towards the general enjoyment of literally boundless wealth." The processes of competition in producing wealth have their origin in the impulse to satisfy desires with the least expenditure of exertion. Competition is the life of trade "in the sense that its spirit or impulse is the spirit or impulse of trade or exchange."[52]

A careful reading of the principles Henry George invoked to establish his basic beliefs about and "methods approach" to political economy provides less than a comprehensive view of his system of economic thought. But it does give a reasonable idea. It also demonstrates that George was methodical and consistent in his thinking. Methodologically, he was a solid, classical economist and perhaps even more than some of them, he took pains to base his analysis on careful, intensive thought processes.

CHAPTER 2

The Life and Economics of Henry George

Introduction

Academic economists usually pursue studies in the field after encountering as a student a university economics class that appealed to them. From there they develop a more specialized interest in one of the formal "fields" of economics, which ultimately becomes their chosen specialty for research and publication.

Because Henry George was not an academic economist, he came to economics as one seeking answers to questions about things that he had seen and experienced. The pursuit of economics was for him no simple process of doing what titillates; rather, he felt compelled to determine why his travels caused him to witness increasing poverty and hardship among the majority of the people at a time when there was significant growth and development going on in America and other industrializing countries. This chapter looks at some of Henry George's experiences[1] and considers how those experiences influenced his intellectual curiosity and ideas, but more importantly the development of the economic theory that made him famous.

The next section will look rather closely at Henry George's fundamental nature and values, revealing the importance of his family and of his religious values. How these values extended into his professional life and efforts will be addressed in the following section. Thereafter, we will inquire as to the life work of George, which he conceived as fighting poverty and elevating the laboring classes, of which he considered himself a part. To some extent, this is an inquiry into George's personal *poverty*. The chapter's final section addresses George's personal progress, reviewing the course of his becoming a political economist and a self-trained scholar.

George's Family and Religious Values

George's father was an Episcopal vestryman, given to faithful Sunday devotions with Church services morning, afternoon, and frequently, evening. A Catholic bishop recalled Henry George going to Church every Sunday, "walking between his two elder sisters, followed by his father and mother— all of them so neat, trim and reserved" (George, Jr., 1900, p. 6). After George left home at an early age, his parents corresponded with him, encouraging him to remember his heritage and his prayers. His mother described in some detail a religious revival that had sparked interest at home and his father assured him that he prayed that God would watch over him until he "brings *all* at last to his eternal kingdom" (p. 86).

As a father in his 50s, Henry George in the company of his son and daughter once saw in New York an undertaker's wagon stop before a residence to deliver armfuls of black drapery. "None of that when I am dead," he told his children. "Death is as natural as life; it means a passage into another life. If a man has lived well—if he has kept the faith—it should be a time for rejoicing, not for repining, that the struggle here is over" (p. 546).

George's belief in immortality, according to his son, was "staunch as a rock." When a friend asked him what he regarded as the strongest evidence of the soul's immortality, he promptly responded, "The creation of human beings is purposeless if this is all." At the funeral of a friend in 1891 George said:

> Ceased to be? No; I do not believe it! Cease to be? No; only to our senses yet encompassed in the flesh that he has shed. For our hearts bear witness to our reason that that which stands for good does not cease to be . . . The changing matter, the passing energy that gave to this body its form are even now on their way to other forms. In a few hours there will remain to our sight but a handful of ashes. But that which we instinctively feel as more than matter and more than energy; that which in thinking of our friends to-day we cherish as best and highest—that cannot be lost. If there be in the world order and purpose, that still lives.
>
> (p. 547)

George, of course, was not a man of the cloth. His life work he saw as being to improve the world, especially in terms of providing accurate conceptions of truth in the realm of economics. His religious spirit is the first part of his life that is addressed here because it was fundamental to Henry George and was a key influence on his work. It must first be observed that as a man of 40 years, in a letter to a friend, a Catholic priest, George could say of himself, "I care nothing of creeds. It seems to me that in any church or out of them one may serve the Master" (p. 311). More importantly, it was his sentiment that "We are here, conscious of things to do. We came here not of ourselves. We must be part of a plan. We have work to perform. If we refuse to go forward with the work here, how do we know but that it shall have to be performed elsewhere" (ibid.). It was this religious conviction that provided his great concern about the poverty of his fellowmen in an economic system that generated progress. He pursued his writings with a commitment and perhaps even a zeal, products of his belief that God had called him, as it were, to reveal fundamental economic truths to his fellowmen. This point will be addressed later, to show more precisely George's view of this professional "calling" he had received. We will return to this when it is time to review his interpretation of God's role in his life's work. Given this orientation, George would have tended to see order in nature and the potential for such in the social order. Divine purpose can be revealed to mankind, but requires individuals endowed with understanding to promote the divine will. George seems to have sensed that he was a part of the Lord's plan to bring harmony and justice to the social order.

This feeling seems evident in a letter that accompanied one of the first copies of *Progress and Poverty*, which Henry sent to his father in 1879. He wrote:

> It is with a deep feeling of gratitude to Our Father in Heaven that I send you a printed copy of this book. I am grateful that I have been enabled to live to write it, and that you have been enabled to live to see it. It represents a great deal of work and a good deal of sacrifice, but now it is done. It will not be recognized at first—maybe not for some time—but it will ultimately be considered a great book, will be published in both hemispheres, and be translated into different languages. This I know, though neither of us may ever see it here. But the belief that I have expressed in this book—the belief that there is yet another life for us makes that of little moment.
>
> (p. 321)

It is evident that George felt a divine influence in his family life. In 1876, in a letter to his wife, George noted something in their relationship that he believed would go beyond the present life. He wrote, "Others may, but it is not for you and me, my darling, to doubt the goodness of God. The more I think of it, the more I feel that our present life will not bound our love" (p. 260). Henry Jr. did not dwell excessively on the strong love that bound his parents together, but he did quote from a small number of George's letters to his beloved wife, revealing his conviction that "Marriage is not only the foundation of society," but it is also that divinely appointed state that can bring the "highest and purest happiness" to people. George did not doubt that if people really understood that they could not separate from each other, "the result would be to make them try harder to live comfortably with each other" (p. 258).

Marriage and many other life experiences brought George to his belief. It wasn't a part of his early years, in spite of his parents' ardent wish that he would find his way to religiosity. In his young years he had shrunk from the "literal acceptance of scriptures" that was taught to him in the family circle. He was loath to inflict injury on the tender spirits of those at home, but he had come "to reject almost completely the forms of religion, and with the forms had cast out belief in a life hereafter" (p. 103). But enthusiastic friends of Methodist persuasion were able to open his mind to serious consideration of religious doctrines.

> When his sister, Jenny, died in 1862, George could not believe that his dear sister was gone. George Jr. would write that his father, with the manner of a sudden conviction, said that there *must* be, there *is* another life—that the soul *is* immortal. But his words expressed his longing, rather than his conviction. Immortality was something he now earnestly wished to believe in. But the theology of his youth did not persuade him, and it was not until many years afterward, when pursuing the great inquiry that produced "Progress and Poverty," that he perceived the "grand simplicity and unspeakable harmony of universal law," that beneficence and intelligence govern social laws, instead of blind, clashing forces; and then faith from reason came and immortality became a fixed belief.
>
> (p. 134)

The Revelation, the Calling

By 1870, having published a number of analytical pieces in recognized newspapers, George had become a familiar name. He knew important people and his opinion was valued. He had become an editor of repute, and he had corresponded with John Stuart Mill, then at the "zenith of his reputation" (p. 208). He had thought a lot about speculation in land and the speculative fever that had seized the populace. The railroad land grants had been a part of the anticipation that swelling populations would hasten the rise in land values.

In this situation and at this stage in his life, George went one afternoon for a ride on horseback. He later described his experience as follows:

> Absorbed in my own thoughts, I had driven the horse into the hills until he panted. Stopping for breath, I asked a passing teamster, for want of something better to say, what land was worth there. He pointed to some cows grazing off so far that they looked like mice and said: "I don't know exactly, but there is a man over there who will sell some land for a thousand dollars an acre." Like a flash it came upon me that there was the reason of advancing poverty with advancing wealth. With the growth of population, land grows in value, and the men who work it must pay more for the privilege. I turned back, amidst quiet thought, to the perception that then came to me and has been with me ever since.
>
> (p. 210)

In his book *The Science of Political Economy,* George returned to this theme of his "calling" with the following expression of his conviction:

> I well recall the day when, checking my horse on a rise that overlooks San Francisco Bay, the commonplace reply of a passing teamster to a commonplace question, crystallized, as by lightning-flash, my brooding thoughts into coherency, and I there and then recognized the natural order—one of those experiences that make those who have had them feel thereafter that they can vaguely appreciate what mystics and poets have called the "ecstatic vision." Yet at that time

I had never heard of the Physiocrats, or even read a line of Adam Smith.

(p. 149)

Even as a young man just short of 30 years of age, George's heart and mind denied that want and suffering were an unalterable part of the nature of things. His son wrote of him that "silently, without telling any man of what he did, he set himself the task of finding the natural order" (p. 192). Years later, George wrote that coming to New York from the West, unknown and knowing nobody, he vowed that he would seek out and remedy, if he could, "the cause that condemned little children to lead such a life as you know them to lead in the squalid districts" (ibid.).

In a letter to a priest and a friend, he wrote in 1883 of something he had previously told no one. "Once in daylight, and in a city street," he wrote, "there came to me a thought, a vision, a call – give it what name you please. But every nerve quivered. And there and then I made a vow. Through evil and through good, whatever I have done and whatever I have left undone, to that I have been true" (p. 193).

George's Own Poverty

At an early age, George had left all formal schooling and set off on a sailing ship to find his destiny. In the following years he had a diversity of experiences, often in the printing field, and he encountered gold fever in California. His financial insecurity, which remained an important part of his young life and extended well into the years of his marriage and family life, naturally caused him to be continually concerned about income and his financial situation. But by the time he had reached his mid-30s, George Jr. tells us that the "dream of wealth, indeed, the desire for it, had long since departed. The dream of increasing the world's happiness and of raising the mass of men out of the slough of poverty had taken its place" (p. 255). The wish to get beyond the anxieties of a hand-to-mouth existence did lead him into mining investments from time to time, when "the atmosphere became surcharged with the mining fever" (ibid.).

But earlier in his life, George came close enough to poverty to have a profound appreciation for its devastation. He had arrived in San Francisco "dead broke" late in 1858 to begin a series of years "notable for a restless pitching about, with shifting scenes of prosperity and adversity" (p. 83).

After his marriage, he struggled financially as a young typesetter, having only irregular work and unsteady income and struggling with debts; he was not always able to pay the rent. Sometimes he earned little, sometimes what he did earn was not paid him. George confesses to his journal that he came near to starving to death, and at one time was saved from that fate by the job of printing a few cards, which enabled him to buy a little cornmeal. It was in these dire straits that George's second child arrived in the family. When the baby boy was born, the doctor instructed them not to pause to wash the child, but to feed him immediately, as he was starving. George went to the office under the necessity of making some money immediately, but "nothing came into the office and he did not know where to borrow" (p. 148). The following events he related only many years later.

> I walked along the street and made up my mind to get money from the first man whose appearance might indicate that he had it to give. I stopped a man – a stranger – and told him I wanted $5. He asked what I wanted it for. I told him that my wife was confined and that I had nothing to give her to eat. He gave me the money. If he had not, I think I was desperate enough to have killed him.
>
> (p. 149)

Henry George narrated this experience to Dr. James E. Kelly, who became his lifelong friend and family physician, attending him at his death bed. This occurred in a conversation in Dublin when George was just over 40, in which George wanted to demonstrate that environment "has more to do with human actions, and especially with so-called criminal actions, than we generally concede" (ibid.). He wished to show how severe poverty may drive normal, moral men to commit deeds that are supposed to be strictly those of hardened, evil natures.

In this period of his greatest poverty, 1865, he saw his distressed state as a function of his own inadequacy, or at least as susceptible to improvement through his own personal efforts. He saw himself start over, embarrassed and crippled with over $200 in debts. His journal received these sentiments: "I wish to profit by my experience and to cultivate those qualities necessary to success in which I have been lacking. I have not saved as much as I ought and am resolved to practice a rigid economy until I have something ahead" (p. 150).

He planned to make every cent he possibly could, to spend nothing unnecessarily, to save something each week, "if only a five cent piece borrowed for the purpose," and not to incur any debt if it could be avoided. Such were the feelings of a struggling soul in a time of challenge and during which society gave no thought to the creation of a social safety net. Things did begin to improve gradually, although work remained for a time scant and irregular. Annie, his wife, paid a month's rent in this period by sewing for her landlady. She remarked to her husband "how contentedly they should be able to live if he could be sure of making regularly twenty dollars a week" (p. 153).

Henry George Jr. recognized that these experiences gave his father the quality of sympathy. He worked throughout his life to improve the state of the laboring class. He could understand the poverty, the grinding labor, and the hopelessness of so many. The biographer wrote:

> He himself had climbed out on swaying yards like the commonest man, carried his blankets as a prospector and common miner, felt something of the hardships of farming,

tramped dusty roads as a pedlar, had every experience as
a printer, and suffered the physical and mental tortures of
hunger. Learning and pride and power and tradition and
precedent went for little with him; the human heart, the
moral purpose, became the core thing.

(pp. 306–07)

George's Own Progress

George's love of the written word led him quite naturally
to his own personal course of study. His interest in public affairs arose from his exposure to them through the
printing business. It was inevitable that he would sooner
or later feel the need to understand economics, since the
question of resource allocation pervades most of the topics
journalists, writers, and politicians must deal with. University economics instructors cannot fail to notice, of course,
how seldom journalism majors enter the doors of their
classrooms, a fact that is clearly reflected in the far from
exceptional quality of economic observation and analysis in
today's news media. George was different, and it is surprising that he actually did something about his ignorance of
economics.

By the time he was 40, George had acquired a library of
nearly 800 volumes, which he considered his chief posses-
sions in the world. They addressed the subjects of political
economy, history and biography, poetry, philosophy, popular science, travels and discovery, "with but few works of
fiction" (p. 302). He most frequently read poetry through
his life, but spent a great deal of time reading and study-
ing (marking passages and taking notes from) the standard
works of political economy. These, he confessed, were the
most challenging of all the things he read.

It had all begun when he was about 19, staying at a
small hotel. Whenever he was not engaged in setting type
at a printing office, a vocation he had just begun, he would

spend time at the hotel's little library, with its several hundred volumes, reading. It was there that he first encountered (but doesn't appear to have begun reading at that point) Adam Smith's *Wealth of Nations*. After another 19 years, George was prepared to comment on Smith's famous treatise and on the nature and state of political economy in the United States. He had begun to write tracts and newspaper editorials of his own.

Because of his readily apparent command of political economy and because of the growing popular influence of his writings, he was ultimately invited to give a lecture at the University of California, Berkeley, on the study of political economy. We will encounter in the chapters that follow a number of the diverse topics in economics and a number of the books George wrote in that period. These writings, along with his newspaper articles and public addresses, had begun to bring him a good deal of notoriety. He was considered by some an appropriate candidate for the chair the University had established in political economy.

The thrust of his message, which clearly could not have endeared him to the academicians who might otherwise have welcomed him into their ranks, was that economics was a subject of far greater simplicity and certainty than generally recognized. George considered it a most important subject, but one that the serious student could readily master on his own with a little informed effort.

In this field's province, he said, are included "all that relate to the wages of labor and the earnings of capital; all regulations of trade; all questions of currency and finance; all taxes and public disbursements – in short, everything that can in any way affect the amount of wealth which a community can secure . . ."

At this juncture, a 100 years after the appearance of Smith's *Wealth*, the science had not yet appeared to make much progress. This was due, George opined, partly to the nature of the science and partly to the way "it was cultivated." Whenever political economy wished to present a scientific principle to the world, it did not have merely general ignorance to deal with. It would also have to expect to counter vested interests "made fierce by passions" (p. 276).

It is not hard to imagine that the academic establishment George addressed was far from delighted with his judgment of their handling of the discipline. He spoke fearlessly:

> Now, while the interests thus aroused furnish the incentive, the complexity of the phenomena with which political economy deals makes it comparatively easy to palm off on the unreasoning all sorts of absurdities as political economy . . . But what is far worse than any amount of pretentious quackery is, that the science even as taught by the masters is in large measure disjointed and determinate. As laid down in the best text-books, political economy is like a shapely statue but half hewn from the rock . . . Strength and subtilty have been wasted in intellectual hair splitting and super-refinements, in verbal discussions and disputes, while the great high-roads have remained unexplored. And thus has been given to a simple and attractive science an air of repellent abstruseness and uncertainty.
>
> (pp. 276–77)

While engaged in the writing of *Progress and Poverty,* struggling momentarily with family finance issues once again, he decided that he should turn to lecturing in the attempt to enhance his income. His ideas on land and land policy had won him a small following of influential people, a number of whom were engaged in the "Land Reform League of California." His lectures attracted few people, but resulted in his being promoted by the League and by others as a delegate to a convention to rewrite the California Constitution. Because he refused to be bound by the planks of the Democratic Party and be under obligation to represent some points of view he did not share, he failed to win this office.

But his engagement in social and intellectual affairs was never to be reversed from this point. As a result of his book and his growing fame within and beyond the borders of the United States, he ultimately became very renowned and lectured to large crowds of sometimes even adoring disciples. He did not rest upon his laurels when the writing of his *magnum opus* was complete. He went on to write many essays and several other books in defense of his principles and beliefs in the field of political economy. He was a classical economist whose works were of a consistent high standard, although they were growing apart from those of the profession generally.

That would not necessarily seem tragic, although George felt it as a tragedy; in his mind the fine principles of political economy were being abandoned. In his *Science of Political Economy* (p. 208), he would finally write:

> Such inquiry as I have been able to make of the recently published works and writings of the authoritative professors of the science has convinced me that this change has been general among all the colleges both of England and the United States. So general is this scholastic utterance that it may now be said that the science of political economy, as founded by Adam Smith and taught authoritatively in 1880, has now been utterly abandoned, its teachings being referred to as teachings of 'the classical school' of political economy, now obsolete.

Some of the notions and "principles" of classical economics that were of little effect in explaining economic phenomena have quietly been laid aside. There have arisen new structures, especially those of neoclassical economics, and "modern" economic theories, which include those of diverse schools and methodologies. These, like classical economics, will last as long as they are useful in understanding and explaining real-world phenomena or in expanding the logical power of abstract conceptualization. The field has become more complex, more inclusive and its dimensions are no longer those established by any single, great mind. Economists do, of course, faithfully recognize the work of individual contributors to any of the schools of economics for any concepts they add to the body of knowledge that remain in use. For a good number of brilliant insights and ideas, Henry George received little appreciation from the profession generally, although he has received a generous measure of credit from specialized historians of economic thought. In addition, George still has followers who are not economists, who wish to live in an intellectual world that George himself once inhabited. Other contemporaries, usually economists, recognize George's healthy and strong influence in the kinds of work in which they are currently engaged.

It is of singular interest that Henry George was not acknowledged—his work was on occasion even spurned— by academic economists of his own day. But it is fair to say, and it is one of the theses of this book, that Henry George's work has been acknowledged in our time by an impressive number of the stellar personalities of the academy. The profession of economics has gradually rehabilitated Henry George's analysis and insights. That they are now seen as a major source of inspiration for several important fields of economics is a central theme of the last two chapters of this book.

An appropriate conclusion to this section of the present chapter was suggested by an observation of one of the anonymous reviewers of this book; it is one for which I am grateful. Although George was such a prominent political economist in California at the time of his Berkeley lecture, and despite his ultimate achievement of national and international renown, he was all but forgotten by the twenty-first century. This may have been due to the fact that George was really preoccupied with the problem of social justice. For him, an understanding of economics was important primarily because, and to the extent that, such understanding was necessary for the establishment of a just social order. By the time he achieved national prominence, formal economics (increasingly academic economics) had become concerned first and foremost with efficiency and had less and less to say about justice. We will see, again and again, in the course of our intellectual tour of George's writings that this was the case.

George and the Burning Issues of His Time

As a publisher and, what was far less significant to his professional life, a part-time politician, George was called upon to address some of the high-profile public policy issues of his time. Addressing these issues one at a time led him quite naturally to recognize in his own views a system of thought appropriately described as classical economics. He was generally quite consistent in the positions he took with the fundamental market principles to which he subscribed.

Had he been an academic economist he would not necessarily have been called upon to take published positions on social policy problems of the day, although he doubtless would have had his own personal views on numerous topics. Normative economics, the economics of what "should be," is not necessarily the terrain of the professional economist. The larger *Gesellschaft* is mostly interested only in the normative views of decorated economists, Nobel Prize winners, et cetera. It once seemed somewhat beneath most economists to go public with personal policy views. More recently, from a historical perspective, the public seems to have become more interested in what even less decorated economists think about economic problems and crises (and there is sometimes a willingness to pay for the economist's views). It is not surprising, therefore, that most economists are now anything but reluctant to share their personal, normative views.

George was in a different profession as publisher, editor, and journalist. His views generally grew in power and respectability with his professional progress and with his increasing understanding of economics. As an instance of this, George corresponded with and published some of the correspondence he had with the British philosopher/ economist John Stuart Mill, the leading classical economist of the time, on the question of imported Chinese labor and its potential effects on the American worker. George and Mill both saw the problem of such labor, basically competing with abundant, unskilled American labor for too few, not very well paid, jobs, as more than an economics issue. In spite of his position on free trade, George was strongly opposed to what some contemporaries would think of as the "outsourcing" of American jobs, although in this case it was to Chinese labor within the United States. The cultural and political implications of the practice were probably more important for George than the economic implications, although his sympathy for the position of the American laborer was strong. He felt that Chinese labor need not be excluded from the United States if the land monopoly question were properly addressed. If land were made available to the workers, wages would increase for domestic labor with the growth of the economy. The demand for cheaper Chinese labor from the "land-grabbers" and land speculators of George's day would disappear, but growth could increase the overall labor demand, providing opportunity for Chinese workers as well.

The fundamental economics principle of free trade represents another example of George's keen interest in economic policy. That principle, of course, implies free markets and mobility not only for commodities, but also for the factors of production, including labor. George had begun as a protectionist, accepting the doctrine on the basis of the respect he had for some of its advocates. Attending a lecture one night in Sacramento before he was 30 years old, he heard the protectionist views of William H. Mills, then Land Agent of the Central Pacific Railroad. George commented:

I was a protectionst when he began, but when he got through I was a free trader. When they asked me what I thought of it I told them that if what he said was true, it seemed to me that the country that was hardest to get at must be the best country to live in; and that, instead of merely putting duties on things brought from abroad, we ought to put them on things brought from anywhere, and that fires and wars and impediments to trade and navigation were the very best things to levy on commerce.

(p. 169)

From that time George never wavered from his classical free trade stance, although his social position on importing Chinese labor (based on cultural and political considerations rather than on economic theory) has the specious appearance of an exception. In all this we should remember that George had deep feelings for justice and less than the neoclassical concern for efficiency in such issues.

The position George took on subsidies of land to the railroads was fully in harmony with his position on free trade generally. In opposing the large land grants to American railroads, he was not in opposition to the development of the railroads or to the regions receiving such land grants. The summary of a pamphlet George wrote on the subject shows clearly the power of his analysis and the values he wished to promote in writing the following:

Railroad subsidies, like protective duties, are condemned by the economic principle that the development of industry should be left free to take its natural direction.

They are condemned by the political principle that government should be reduced to its minimum – that it becomes more corrupt and more tyrannical, and less under the control of the people, with every extension of its powers and duties.

They are condemned by the Democratic principle which forbids the enrichment of one citizen at the expense of another; and the giving to one citizen of advantages denied to another.

They are condemned by the experience of the whole country which shows that they have invariably led to waste, extravagance and rascality; that they inevitably become a source of corruption and a means of plundering the people.

The only method of preventing the abuse of subsidies is by prohibiting them altogether.

(pp. 216–17)

George was convinced that the elimination of the railroad land subsidies would provide more stimulus by far than the subsidies. If the protective duty imposed on the iron used to build the railroads were removed, the cost of building them would be reduced many thousand dollars per mile. The stimulus that the reduction of taxation would give to the industry of the whole country would create a new demand for railroads and vastly increase the growth of industry.

George was best known for his views on land policy. His theory emphasized land speculation and monopolization; as landholders collected increasing rents, the returns to labor didn't reflect the growth of population, the improvements in technology, and the increasing capital stock. It was his conviction, of course, that the use of the land, like its ownership, should be for all people. If the land of a country were owned only by a small class, George worried, that class would rule the country. Nevertheless, no confiscation of land need be undertaken if policymakers are astute enough simply to impose a tax on it. That would take away the advantage of speculative landholding and force unused land to be put to profitable use. George believed that the tax revenues from the land tax could replace all other tax revenues, so that all other taxation could disappear. He dedicated long passages to showing how many amazingly good things could happen as the result of a single tax on land.

Although George's theories can be reviewed by reference to a multitude of sources, George Jr., his biographer, reviewed them competently (pp. 225–30). The first expression of George's basic economic ideas appeared in a small-type, 48-page pamphlet he published under the title *Our Land and Land Policy*. Land, George instructed, should be parceled out to actual settlers in small quantities without charge. We should fund government activities with a tax on the land's value (it is of great importance that this *did not include improvements to the value of the land*), which would add nothing to prices or the cost of living, costing the general voters nothing. The land by right belongs to all the people, rather than merely to those who historically, through various means, have confiscated it from those who hold no land. Landholders would simply be taxed for the value of the land actually held. Since land cannot be hidden or moved, the land tax can be collected with more ease and certainty, and at less expense than any other tax. It cannot be shifted from the landowner to someone else.

George was inordinately pleased to learn later that the French physiocrats, known to their French contemporaries simply as *économistes,* under François Quesnay, from whom Adam Smith had learned a great deal, had also (and for similar reasons) advocated a single land tax, the *impot unique.* It was after the publication of his views on land policy that George encountered Adam Smith and other classical economists under the influence of the Physiocrats. He mastered their writings and felt that he had simply rediscovered the truths of classical economics independently.[2]

George has been "misunderstood" by individuals who were tempted to misrepresent his motives and discredit him by alleging that he demanded confiscation of private lands. It is true that George could have argued eloquently and cogently for such a policy, but he was not interested in social revolution. His policy of the single tax obviated the need for anything like nationalization of land. In his pamphlet, George wrote:

> While it is true that the land of a country is the free gift of the Creator to all the people of that country, to the enjoyment of which each has an equal natural right, it is also true that the recognition of private ownership in land is necessary to its proper use – is, in fact, a condition of civilisation. When the millennium comes, and the old savage, selfish instincts have died out of men, land may perhaps be held in common; but not till then.
>
> (p. 233)

Let us conclude this discussion with reference to a major oration by George on July 4, 1877, when he was 38 years old. The thoughts, expressed with very little change, later became a part of *Progress and Poverty* and they reflected George's deepest feelings on the subject of liberty and economics (p. 286).

> We speak of Liberty as one thing, and of virtue, wealth, knowledge, invention, national strength, and national independence as other things. But, of all these, Liberty is the source, the mother, the necessary condition. She is to virtue what light is to color, to wealth what sunshine is to grain; to knowledge what eyes are to the sight. She is the genius of invention, the brawn of national strength, the spirit of national independence! Where Liberty rises, there virtue grows, wealth increases, knowledge expands, invention multiplies human powers, and in strength and spirit the freer nation rises among her neighbours as Saul amid his brethren – taller and fairer. Where Liberty sinks, there virtue fades, wealth diminishes, knowledge is forgotten, invention ceases, and empires once mighty in arms and arts become a helpless prey to freer barbarians!

George understood and taught in exceptionally clear and sometimes stirring language what self-styled patriots so often appear to forget. Free men pursue their own material interests. With free institutions and free markets, their powerful incentives to build a good life for themselves and their families engage them in hard work and creative efforts to produce what their neighbors badly want and are willing to pay for. This creative effort need not include the pursuit of antisocial ends, but should they arise, such pursuits can be discouraged by institutional sanctions on inappropriate, opportunistic behavior, sanctions on taking advantage of others to achieve strictly personal interests. Many of those who believe in the institutions of free markets carry the conviction that free societies tend to produce people of more altruistic inclinations than arise under the want and social dysfunctionality so commonly associated with tyranny.

CHAPTER 3

Henry George's Theory
of Distribution

Introduction

This chapter reviews Henry George's theory of distribution from the perspective of his *magnum opus, Progress and Poverty*. This work is not only good reading, it had a powerful impact on the economic/social discussions of his time and produced echoes that linger to the present. It was not, of course, a work that provided him admission to the economics establishment of his day. At the time, economists were less inclined to find redeeming qualities to his theories than contemporary economists are.

Evaluation of the work as a contribution to the development of economic analysis cannot be done in a vacuum; it must be measured against the leading works of its time. Space constraints, however, make it impossible to make more than the most essential comparisons with other works of that age.

The choices for comparison seem obvious. The first will be Alfred Marshall's writings, which from an academic standpoint became the most important competition for George's popular book. Marshall became the first of the neoclassical economists; his work bridged the classical era and the new era he introduced at Cambridge. George may have contributed the best classical analysis in history, but it was Marshall who constructed the bridge from the classical to the contemporary world of economics.[1] Part of understanding what George did is realizing what he did not do, namely, produce his economic theory in a more contemporary methodological format, as Marshall did.

A number of other choices for comparison recommend themselves, including the second choice of Francis Amasa Walker, the leading academic economist in George's America. Walker's works were not to become a permanent part of economics as Marshall's would, yet he was the spokesman for American academic economists. Walker, having been scorned and ridiculed by George himself, remained unshakably determined to keep George in the nether regions of the outsider.

A comparison of George with Marshall and Walker will help us put the former into historical context, but we will also want to introduce more contemporary views of George. We don't expect George to be timelessly powerful or timelessly "correct," but in the light of improved theory and with the greater objectivity of passing decades, we can hope to come to a more dispassionate understanding of George's contribution. We wish to know how George is viewed by those who produce the best economics available historically, and most of history's greatest economists are still alive, although many important contributors will gradually be passing from the scene.

It turns out that despite the rancor of most of the evaluations of George's work during his lifetime, his contribution was a powerful one. Aside from the fact that he had more impact on an international reading public and on the political developments of his own time than did his contemporaries, Henry George was also an important actor, one of the final great ones, in the field of classical economics. Self-taught and gifted in written expression, he might have been viewed as the American father of classical economics, while the stars of the school historically featured mostly British and European figures. He was not associated with the American academy, being alienated by both the academy's refusal of recognition and his own choice. Part of the motivation of this study is to consider why George is not generally viewed as the father of American economics when he held such a lofty place among the few gifted early American economists.

This review of the George contribution will begin with his proffered theory of distribution, then move to a comparison of Marshall's basic theory and a discussion of Walker's work. This implies a comparison of the classical and neoclassical approaches to the theory of distribution, ultimately transformed by Marshall into a theory of factor prices. The discussion will conclude with a review of the judgments of some great "contemporary" economists who have written about George and his works. They are "contemporary" because they include the great minds (such as Joseph Schumpeter, a half-century immortal who rightly claims membership in the group) whose writings and viewpoints make up the basic canon by which contemporary economists are educated.

George's Theory of Distribution

For the uninitiated, it will be helpful to begin our discussion of the theory of distribution with an explanation of the term "distribution." Distribution explains how total output or income is distributed among the factors of production as wages for labor, rent for land, and interest for capital. In each of the separate markets, the prices of the productive factors, including wages, rent, and interest, are the result of the forces of supply and demand for those factors. Distribution theory is the fundamental approach of economics to the question of how the system works. It explains how the factors of production interact to produce and to share the national product; it tells us how the economic system performs in terms of efficiency and gives us some important hints as to the social justice the system provides.

George began, as did the economists of his age, with the largely agricultural and gradually developing, nascent industrial economy based upon the productive contributions and returns to the factors of land, capital, and labor. He looked at the price of grain grown on land of the highest quality, including the costs of wages and interest. The market price of grain must cover not only the cost of grain grown on the highest quality land, but also the higher costs incurred on plots of lesser quality or fertility.

Whenever the market price is more than enough to cover the costs of wages and interest on the highest quality land, costs which Henry George refers to as "the margin of cultivation," a rent will accrue to those fortunate landlords. The price just covering wages and interest on land of the best quality is also referred to by Henry George as "the rent line."

> Wealth produced in every community is divided into two parts by what may be called the rent line, which is fixed by the margin of cultivation, or the return which labor and capital could obtain from such natural opportunities as are free to them without the payment of rent. From the part of the produce below this line wages and interest must be paid. All that is above goes to the owners of land.[2]

Interest, of course, accrues to capital, which is defined as "all wealth used to produce more wealth." Labor is all human exertion, and its return in distribution is called wages.

George and the Wages Fund

According to classical economic theory, the "political economy" of George's time, wages were seen as fixed by the ratio of laborers to the amount of capital devoted to the employment of labor, the so-called wages fund. Classical economists conceived of production as a problem of employing workers before they had produced any output with which they could be paid. Current wages would be drawn from advances of capital accumulated before the production cycle began. The actual wage depended on the size of the fund divided by the number of workers employed. Wages were also believed to exhibit a tendency to the "lowest amount on which laborers will consent to live and reproduce."[3]

But if wages were a function of the quantity of labor employed and the capital devoted to its employment, the classical mind would infer that high wages, the product of scarce labor, must be accompanied by low interest, the product of abundant capital. Or if abundant labor produced low wages, high interest would arise from the scarcity of capital relative to that labor. George completely rejected this conclusion just as he did the wages fund theory itself. He wrote of "a general truth that interest is high where and when wages are high, and low where and when wages are low?"[4]

Part and parcel of George's rejection of the wages fund theory was his conclusion that wages, rather than being derived from a wages fund, that is, an advance provided by capital, are actually paid from labor's output. On this point, George wrote with the very practical simplicity of the producer.

> Make an exact inventory of his capital on Monday morning before the beginning of work, and it will consist of his buildings, machinery, raw materials, money on hand, and finished products in stock. Suppose, for the sake of simplicity, that he neither buys nor sells during the week, and after work has stopped and he has paid his hands on Saturday night, take a new inventory of his capital. The item of money will be less, for it has been paid out in wages; there will be less raw material, less coal, etc., and a proper deduction must be made from the value of the buildings and machinery for the week's wear and tear. But if he is doing a remunerative business, which must on the average be the case, the item of finished products will be so much

greater as to compensate for all these deficiencies and show in the summing up an increase of capital. Manifestly, then, the value he paid his hands in wages was not drawn from his capital, or from any one else's capital. It came, not from capital, but from the value created by the labor itself. There was no more advance of capital than if he had hired his hands to dig clams, and paid them with a part of the clams they dug.[5]

Some have seen in George's criticisms of the wages fund an important insight that production is a continuous process in opposition to the traditional view of classical economics that it is a point-input, point-output process. Naturally, the inflexible "yearly harvest" notion of the earlier classical economists is not an inalienable requirement of the wages fund theory. Historically, some economists have seemed more understanding of the fumbling analysis of the earlier wages fund economists than of George's early insight that production theory should be based upon a continuous production function.[6]

Some later economists were prepared to supply a beating to George for failing to prove *mathematically* the inadequacy of the wages fund doctrine. The debate continued for some time after J. S. Mill made an initial recantation of the wages fund, causing others to come to the defense of the theory. A contemporary evaluation is contributed by Samuelson,[7] who suggests that modern economists should understand that the wages fund should not be "confused with the totality of circulating capital" and that it is the "malleable *result* of the equilibrium process and not a *causal* determinant of the level of the real wage in any meaningful long run, intermediate run, or short run."[8]

Marshall seems largely to have avoided the whole issue by moving beyond the wages fund and, rather than attacking the idea, quietly failing to employ it in his writings. The concept fails to receive mention in the two chapters on a "Preliminary Survey of Distribution" and again in the two chapters on the "Earnings of Labor" in Marshall's Book VI on Distribution. He emphasizes the labor market's forces of supply and demand as the basis of wage theory, completely ignoring the wages fund. He does, of course, dedicate a brief appendix to the wages fund theory, paying lip service to the idea that it undergirds contemporary thought on wages, although his own analysis demonstrates it does not. His relative kindness to the theory may have been in part a slap at Henry George himself, since Marshall well knew of George's objections to it. He restates the proposition simply, observing that "when anyone works for hire, his wages are, as a rule, advanced to him out of his employer's capital – advanced, that is, without waiting till the things which he is engaged in making are ready for use." He then admits that these "simple statements have been a good deal criticized" (a reference to George) "but they have never been denied by anyone who has taken them in the sense in which they were meant." Whether or not denied, it does make sense simply to ignore the theory, since production and wages can quite adequately be analyzed without building on wages fund foundations.

In Appendix J of his Principles of Economics, Marshall (1920) claims of the "vulgar" form of the wages fund theory that "the amount of wages payable in a country is fixed by the capital in it." According to Marshall, that statement cannot be inferred from the conclusion that in agricultural produce, where there is but a single harvest annually, "if all the wheat raised at one harvest is sure to be eaten before the next, and if none can be imported, then it is true that if anyone's share of the wheat is increased, there will be just so much less for others to have." The vulgar form of the theory suggested to "the old economists," Marshall explains,

> that the amount of wages was limited by the amount of capital, and this statement cannot be defended... It has suggested to some people the notion that the total amount

of wages that could be paid in a country in the course of, say a year, was a fixed sum. If by the threat of a strike, or in any other way, one body of workmen got an increase of wages, they would be told that in consequence other bodies of workmen must lose an amount exactly equal in the aggregate to what they had gained.[9]

The issue has also been addressed in terms of fixed and circulating capitals, and some are convinced that it should be resolved by mathematics rather than straightforward logic. Paul Samuelson, the patriarch of contemporary economic theory, notes that Frank Taussig's *Wages and Capital* (1896) was hailed by the famous Jacob Viner, Samuelson's teacher, as a successful vindication of a qualified wage fund— "and even as a successful refutation of Henry George's muddled notion that production in a steady state can be validly regarded as being timeless and synchronized."[10] But Samuelson graciously adds in a footnote: "A referee reminds me that such great scholars as John Bates Clark (1907) and Frank Knight (1934) also displayed the Henry George muddle that confused steady-state surface appearances with timeless synchronization of production."[11] Henry George does not fare worse in the Samuelson analysis than other great economists of his age who were helping develop the neoclassical paradigm. Samuelson respectfully continues the classical debate on some unfinished theoretical issues that need not detain us further here.

Returns to Labor and Capital

Having proceeded to develop George's theory of distribution by reviewing his approach to the wages fund theory, we are now ready to forge on with a consideration of the economic returns to labor, capital, and land á la George, and then on through the basic economic theory of *Progress and Poverty*.[12] George can be read and understood by educated readers, whether or not they have any formal background in economics. The exposition of this chapter attempts not to become too thorny for such readers. To make it more palatable to those who are familiar with economics at the principles level, an appendix is provided with illustrations that you will have encountered in any introductory college course. Should you not yet have experienced anything so delightful, or should you have forgotten what you experienced in an economics course taken some years ago, I would suggest that you take the simpler route of reviewing the descriptive material that follows, just noting the basic relationships and conclusions involved in George's perception of the market economy. To enjoy the flavor of George's views expressed in his own words, you may turn to the appendix at the end of this chapter and find a nice summary of George's analysis by the master himself.

Nonspecialized readers with no experience in economics can skip the appendix with its simple geometry and equations without significant loss. They are designed for the edification of those who refuse to be intimidated. George had a reasonably accurate idea of what noneconomists should find in his analysis, since he was one himself. Carefully thinking through this chapter and his summary in the appendix will arm you with sufficient knowledge for the discussion of his conflict with some of the economists of his day.

George lumps labor and capital together as recipients of a single share or proportion in the national distribution, the other share accruing to land. Labor and capital received wages and interest for their contribution to production, while land received rent. He argued that the market mechanism would keep the wage/interest proportion of national income roughly constant and wages and interest would rise and fall together. He expressed the idea simply:

> For if wages fall, interest must also fall in proportion, else it becomes more profitable to turn labor into capital than to

apply it directly; while, if interest falls, wages must likewise proportionately fall, or else the increment of capital would be checked.[13]

So when wages are low, interest must fall as well, otherwise, producers will hire labor not only as a substitute for capital, but also to produce more of the higher-return capital. Conversely, if interest declines, wages must do so likewise, otherwise, capital would cease to be accumulated because of the lower returns it would offer investors relative to those of labor. A decline in interest would also reduce the proportion of capital's share in distribution because some capital would be diverted from productive to nonproductive uses because of its lower returns. According to George, as the "margin of cultivation" declines, that is, as wages and interest decline, or as the costs of agricultural production on the land decline, the share accruing to rent must increase.

Speculation in land also affects this model by reducing the margin of cultivation, that is, the share of wages and interest in the national output. In George's words, "the speculative advance in land values tends to press the margin of cultivation, or production, beyond its normal limit, thus compelling labor and capital to accept of a smaller return, or (and this is the only way they can resist the tendency) to cease production."[14] Thus, in the course of "progress," wages and interest decline and rent increases inexorably.

There is a functional relationship between population growth, the expansion of land use, and the growth of rent, the return to the factor land. Social progress for George implies both a growing population and increasing land use, the latter phenomenon accommodating larger populations and reflecting land-intensive social activities. As we have seen, while rent increases with social "progress," wages and interest drift downward.

Social forces automatically encourage population growth, implying greater land use as a concomitant. This is to be

expected despite the fact that more capital-intensive production promotes greater output through the adoption of
new labor-saving techniques. In this process, investment is
a function of growth and development along with increasing population and land use. In George's words, "the effect
of inventions and improvements in the productive arts is
to save labor—that is, to enable the same result to be
secured with less labor, or a greater result with the same
labor."[15]

When economic development and technical change
(generally in the form of industrialization and more sophisticated agricultural mechanization) encourage more capital-
intensive production, managers will move in that direction.
Greater labor-saving investments accompany increasing
population and land use. Labor and capital together, including the labor-saving technologies provided in the latter,
cause the returns of all factors to increase.

On labor-saving innovations, George further writes,
"while the primary effect of labor-saving improvements is to
increase the power of labor, the secondary effect is to extend
cultivation, and, where this lowers the margin of cultivation,
to increase rent."[16]

Progress implies population growth, which in turn means
increasing land use. These together cause an increase in the
capital stock and labor-saving innovations and a growth in
national production. This permits workers and capital to
enjoy greater factor returns, and the workers, noticing their
greater prosperity, adopt a lifestyle that also uses more land.

Unfortunately, this economic growth and progress results
in increased factor returns only in the short run. In the
long run, the margin of cultivation declines again; in other
words, wages and interest ultimately decline. However, as
we would expect in a Georgian view of the universe, rent
increases. George argued that the long-run tendency to
increasing land use does not exclude land use by successful workers, some of whom apparently become landowners

as these developments produce progress. George summarizes this process as follows:

> But labor cannot reap the benefits which advancing civiliza-
> tion thus brings, because they are intercepted. Land being
> necessary to labor, and being reduced to private ownership,
> every increase in the productive power of labor but increases
> rent — the price that labor must pay for the opportunity to
> utilize its powers; and thus all the advantages gained by the
> march of progress go to the owners of land, and wages do
> not increase.[17]

For George, land speculation was an inherent part of the process of development. His negative view of the process assumed that the share of rent in national income would increase partly as a result of the speculation that accompanies economic development and diminishes the returns to capital and labor. It is the reduction of the earnings of wages and interest that produces the downside of the business cycle. Moreover, as speculators withhold land from productive use, they curtail production. And Marshall was basically in agreement with this point in his *Principles*, admitting that "antisocial" forms of speculation posed a potential threat to economic progress. At the same time, Marshall did not fail to see the positive, market functions of speculation.[18]

Marshall on George and the Theory of Distribution

Marshall saw his own doctrine as an extension of classical theory. He perceived George's attack on classical theory generally as a distortion of the theory. In fact, both George and Marshall were extending classical theory, but Marshall was extending it into the modern theory that undergirds much of contemporary economics. The Georgian extension simply did not bridge the classical and contemporary eras.

When Marshall "built upon" classical theory, he did not hesitate to demonstrate its inadequacies, thereby establishing the need for his own innovations. When George wrote of such inadequacies, Marshall instinctively defended the classical doctrines.

When Marshall analyzed distribution in his *Principles,* he began by noting how French and English writers over the past century had "represented value as governed almost wholly by cost of production, demand taking a subordinate place."[19] Their results would not be far from the mark, Marshall observed, in a stationary state. He intended to demonstrate what corrections would have to be made to harmonize their results with the actual conditions of life and work. That would largely be to explicate the implications of the demand for labor.

Marshall was proposing that we see returns to factors of production not as the outcomes of macro processes in which factor shares interact somehow, as though at an aggregate level, to determine the distribution of the national income. In George's simple model as presented above this sentiment appears in the classical simplification of making bundled rent and interest a function not of the individual markets that actually determine prices and quantities but simply of the aggregate of land rent. In contemporary economics, each factor's share in national income is the aggregate of what happens in individual factor markets. Forces of both supply and demand prevailing in those markets determine prices, quantities, and aggregate shares.

Contemporary macroeconomics is based upon just such an understanding. The microeconomic foundations of factor markets establish aggregates of the factor returns in national income. In classical economics, individual markets were generally overlooked and factor shares were seen as some simple division of the total product. For George, labor's wages and capital's interest were residuals after the landlords collected their rent. For Marshall, they were a product of the individual factor markets' underlying factor returns.

George perceived rent to be a very special case since the factor land was nonreproducible and strictly limited in supply. By contrast, Marshall wanted to demonstrate that the returns to all productive factors have in common the same basic principles that determine prices in both commodity and factor markets. Those markets differ in specific ways, of course, but their common characteristics make outcomes analogous and predictable.

It is commonly understood today, first, that the cost of an input will be an opportunity cost, that is, an input must be paid what it can earn in its most remunerative alternative employment. This opportunity cost is the factor's transfer earnings. Second, any earnings in excess of a factor's transfer price constitute rent. If the supply of a productive resource were strictly limited and it could be used in only one productive employment, transfer earnings would be zero and the entire return would count as rent. Since, in reality, no agent is incapable of being reproduced or of being adapted to other productive tasks, we must look at the time frame in which such flexibility is to be achieved. Blaug points out that fixed capital earns quasi-rents rather than interest in the short run, since in that time frame the supply of machines can neither be augmented nor adapted to other productive processes. It is clear that in the long run, however, new machines can be employed and old machines modified to perform new tasks, so "quasi-rents are always in the process of being eroded."[20] Thus, other factors of production earn quasi-rents on the same basis that land earns rent.

Neoclassical economics no longer recognizes any need for special treatment of the factor land or for a theory of ground rent.[21] On this basis, Marshall's objection to the "single tax" becomes sensible. It is that *all* productive factors, not simply land, earn short-term "rents." Even Ricardo's long-run differential rents are incentive payments that encourage

economical use of fertile and increasingly scarce land. Blaug quite fairly observes that George might have responded to this Marshallian reasoning by asserting "that no quasi-rent has either the persistence or the generality of ground rent, and Marshall would probably have agreed with that."[22] In the world of pure theory, the existence of quasi-rents may make the analysis of all factors comparable. In practice, there often seems reason to consider land a productive resource with unique qualities.

But Marshall developed his analysis of land rents in a world in which individual markets determined prices and quantities, which were then aggregated into factor shares without the cryptic macro relationships of the classical world. Thus, factor returns could be seen as an aggregate of individual market decisions made by managers engaged in productive processes. Marshall refers to "the alert business man" striving to find

> the most profitable application of his resources, and endeavouring to make use of each several agent of production up to that margin, or limit, at which he would gain by transferring a small part of his expenditure to some other agent; and how he is thus, so far as his influence goes, the medium through which the principle of substitution so adjusts the employment of each agent that, in its marginal application, its cost is proportionate to the additional net product resulting from its use.[23]

Marshall felt that George's theory confused cause and effect. According to George, lower average wages are caused by changes in the value of land in the course of economic progress. In contrast, Marshall explains wage changes on the basis of the theory of competitive markets. In contemporary parlance, as producers strive to minimize production costs, they will watch factor prices and try to balance the ratios of marginal factor productivity to factor prices across all factors of production. This amounts to saying that for any factor of

production, the producer is interested in both how much total costs increase with the purchase of an additional unit of a factor and how much an additional unit of that factor will add to total revenues. Marshall outlined this theory in early lectures he gave in the 1880s on George's already popular work *Progress and Poverty*, but it was in the *Principles of Economics* (1890) that he fully developed his theory of competitive markets.[24] Marshall teaches that "the principle of substitution so adjusts the employment of each agent that, in its marginal application, its cost is proportionate to the additional net product resulting from its use."[25]

Marshall presented his own version of factor pricing in Note XIV of the *Principles*,[26] which for those who have already been exposed to the basics of calculus and its use in economics[27] is discussed in Part II of the appendix to this chapter.

Marshall treated different kinds of labor to be used in constructing a home as one variable and different kinds of rooms for the home as another. Total outlays for the productive factors used in the home's construction were a third variable. The benefit or utility anticipated from the rooms to be constructed was a function of the rooms to be constructed. Total receipts to be derived from sales of the rooms to be produced by the labor factor could also be determined on the basis of the calculus Marshall used for the analysis. His equations represent a balance of effort and benefit. The real cost to the producer of some small additional amount of labor employed to cut and process timber will be neatly balanced by the benefit accruing to the completed product.

If the principal represented here analytically should decide to pay a carpenter instead of doing the work himself, the analysis will determine not the personal total effort involved, but his expenditures for the labor he will employ. In that instance, the rate of pay the carpenters will receive for their additional effort (the agent's marginal demand price for their labor) can likewise be calculated, as well as the

monetary value to the principal of the marginal utilities of extra rooms constructed, or his marginal demand prices for them. According to the equations, the demand price for the carpenters' labor will tend to be equal to the demand price for extra rooms in the home, being multiplied for each room by the marginal efficiency of the carpenters' work in providing that extra accommodation.

Generalizing this statement, the marginal demand price for hired labor is the marginal efficiency of the labor times the marginal demand price for the product. In other words, wages tend to be equal to the value of the output produced, that is, the marginal efficiency of a unit of the labor times the value of the additional product generated. Marshall referred to this as the "net product" of the labor employed. He declares this proposition to be very important, containing "within itself the kernel of the demand side of the theory of distribution."[28]

We would express this today in a form that Marshall would have understood immediately. For the competitive case, the value of the marginal product of input a will tend to an equality with the wage of input a. More generally, the value of the marginal product of any input will be equal to the price (cost) of that input.

As we saw above, the value of the marginal product of input a is VMP_a (the price of X times the marginal product of input a, MP_a). The firm's optimization is achieved by setting the value of the marginal product of a factor equal to the factor's wage, $VMP_a = w_a$. For imperfectly competitive industries, the marginal revenue product, MRP_a, is defined as the marginal revenue of the output, MR_x, times the marginal product of input a, so that $MRP_a = MR_x(MP_a)$. The only difference between the competitive and imperfectly competitive cases being the use of p_x in competition (equal to marginal cost for an optimization of net revenue) and MR_x in imperfect competition (which is lower than p_x and in this case is equated to marginal cost in the stead of the price). Marshall equates the marginal cost of hiring input 1 to the marginal revenue product of that input. These are very contemporary expressions of economic principles.

Note that the inputs or factors of production are interchangeable. The market for each one operates rather independently of the markets of other inputs. Land adds to production as do other inputs and is not treated differently from them. The demand for an input is a derived demand, derived from the demand for the product that the input helps produce. In short, the Marshallian theory has merely been tweaked, that is, it has been clothed in modern notation and presented in more restrictive form to characterize the value to a firm of a factor's output as marginal productivity times the market price (or in cases of imperfect competition, the marginal revenue).

In my view, this contribution of Marshall's, combined with those of other participants in the marginalist "revolution," toward the development of neoclassical theory adds to our theoretical understanding of the issues of distribution in the economy, but is not to be compared to the rather linear progress of science in many other areas. There is no agreement in economics that the neoclassical theory of distribution assures the ultimate and final state of our understanding of both the contribution and the rewards of the productive factors. These achievements are certainly clever and intellectually satisfying, but it is not apparent that they are vastly superior to the kinds of changes that George was offering for the classical model with his rejection of the wages fund theory, the Malthusian population ideas, and so on.

Where Has Distribution Theory Gone since Marshall's Lifetime?

The marginal productivity theory of distribution that grew out of Marshall's writings was also explicated by others who helped establish neoclassical theory. In the 1870s, a new marginal utility paradigm was developed by Jevons, Menger, and Walras, and was followed in the 1880s by marginal productivity theories developed by Clark, Wicksteed, and Wicksell. It was not intended that the previous section suggest the inference that Marshall single-handedly established the marginal productivity theory of neoclassical economics as a full-blown, contemporary economic theory.

It is important to observe that contemporary theory continues to debate the question of income distribution and has yet to reach peremptory agreement on the subject. The debate seemed to peak (achieve a local maximum) in the 1960s with the so-called capital controversy between the Cambridge schools (in England and at MIT, respectively). There are diverse versions of the classical, the neoclassical, and the neo-Keynesian (not to mention Marxian) theories of distribution and all the controversial issues have not yet been resolved. One may respect the position that it is not yet absolutely certain that modern or neoclassical economics has been conclusively demonstrated to be superior to classical distribution theory or the theory of Henry George.

Today, the neoclassical theory we owe to Marshall and others is seen as flawed in two respects. First, marginal productivity seems to have a limited content and narrow conclusions as compared with classical theory.[29] Second, there is an aggregation problem. Productivity theory fits well for the factors hired by a single firm, but when neoclassical economists talk about the level of employment and wages for the aggregate economy, it is as though the whole economy were simply one giant firm. This is inappropriate because aggregate supply and demand are interdependent, so that the theory is forced to assume a given level of income prevailing throughout the economy. Consider the problem as follows.

A single firm's demand for labor is given by the marginal productivity curve for that labor. Labor's industry-wide demand curve is given by summing horizontally the individual firms' demand curves. The next step would logically be to sum all the industry demand curves to get the market demand for labor, since that would imply that the market demand curve and the product demand curves were independent of each other. A little reflection will make it apparent that workers' demand for products will depend on their wages. Changes in wages would change incomes, and therefore, the demands for products. The independence also goes the other way; should the demand for products change, that would impact the demand for workers and in turn affect wages. The upshot is that because of the interdependence of the demand for factors and the demand for products, as well as the interdependence of wages and prices, we don't really have a determinate system. The theory must therefore adopt as an essential hypothesis that consumer demand curves are *not* dependent upon the prices paid to the factors of production.

The problem translates into a macro riddle that disturbed Keynes and set the profession off in search of a Keynesian theory of distribution. The classical economists had argued that in the case of an economic crisis, full employment could be retained by cutting wages. With labor cheaper, more labor would be hired and the cycle would be overcome. But Keynes objected that wage cutting wasn't necessarily a remedy for unemployment. When the economy experiences an excess supply of labor, marginal productivity theory would suggest that wage payments were in excess of the marginal product of labor in some part of the labor market. That would, indeed, suggest cutting wages, but Keynes pointed out once again that wages are not only costs, they are incomes as well. If wages fall generally, that will also reduce the aggregate demand for commodities and services, so there is no guarantee that cutting wages will restore the economy to full employment.

Keynes was not the only critic of the theory. Sraffa and Robinson, both of England's Cambridge, argued that the measurement of capital was a serious problem. The analysis of that problem ultimately revealed internal inconsistencies in the neoclassical theory. That theory defines capitalist income as the product of the profit (or interest) rate and the amount of capital used. But the measurement of the quantity of capital used requires an aggregation of quite heterogeneous physical objects. The neoclassical economists had assumed that one could simply add up the monetary value of those items, but Robinson[30] pointed out that such a financial measurement of capital depended in turn on the rate of profit.

The problem of circularity here can be understood by imagining what would happen in this process if wages were to fall and the return to capital were to rise, which would alter the distribution of income between labor and capital. The result would be a change in the distribution of demand, which would lead to changed prices. The new prices would be associated with a different set of capital goods required to produce the changed bundle of products now in demand. Again, the new set of demands would reflect a different set of preferences, those of capital owners whose share of total income would now be greater. Their tastes and greater incomes would affect new production patterns. So a change in the rate of profit could dramatically change the measured amount of capital. In other words, changing the wage rate or interest rate could change the choice of technique.

A basic proposition of the neoclassical distribution theory, as expressed by Böhm Bawerk, Wicksell, and others,[31] was that there was a simple, monotonic relationship between capital and the rate of profit or interest. A decline in the rate of profit would imply an increase in the amount of capital used. The conceptually very real possibility of capital reswitching suggested by Robinson and Sraffa[32] questioned this relationship. The idea of reswitching was that as the rate of interest fell, the firm would adapt by changing its stock of capital. But then as the rate of interest continued to fall, the firm could actually switch back to the original capital employed.

The potential internal consistency can be expressed in this way. Originally the firm had a marginal productivity of capital MP_{k1} and interest rate i_1, so we had the typical MP/P ratio, MP_{k1}/i_1. This is defined as the inverse of marginal cost and, when equated to the inverse of marginal revenue, we have the firm's basic optimality condition. But when the rate of interest or profit declines, the firm would use a different capital stock and experience its associated marginal productivity of capital, so that we have MP_{k2}/i_2. If reswitching occurs, the firm moves back to the original stock of capital employed and recaptures that stock's MP_{k1}, although it is now at the third and lowest rate of interest and we have MP_{k1}/i_3. Note that in this instance the firm has adopted only two sets of capital, K_1 and K_2, the first one being adopted a second time after the reswitching. When the interest rate falls to i_3, the neoclassical theory would prescribe using more capital, but, inconsistently, the firm instead uses less capital. It returns to the smaller amount of capital that had been applied with the original production techniques, and that capital again yields MP_{k1}.

Paul Samuelson, the neoclassical theoretician who conceded that the reswitching phenomenon made it inconsistent to use an aggregative neoclassical production function for the analysis of capital, moved on to use general equilibrium theory rather than an aggregate production function.

This review of the capital controversy is designed merely to show, first, that although Alfred Marshall brought economics into the modern era, moving the profession away from the classical theory of distribution, he certainly did not do so single-handedly. Second, it hopes to show that the theory Marshall helped to launch has not been viewed by economists as the final word in the progress of economics, especially given the technical, internal inconsistencies associated with its analysis of capital.

Whatever theory of distribution ultimately prevails is not the important issue for our purposes. Henry George was not a part of the discussion that took the world from classical to more modern conceptual constructs. That is certainly not all bad. Some economists today are inclined to think that the inconsistencies in neoclassical distribution theory require a reconstruction of economic theory from its very foundations. Others would favor a "resumption and development of the more comprehensive approach of the classical economists."[33] So the old approach can be seen as having something to recommend it. George was using the more generally applied analysis of his day, and his use was neither inept nor inappropriate. He was not at the cutting edge of economic theory, but at that time even the cutting edge (as even today) still had a fair piece to go.[34]

George's Policy Proposals

Having already developed his notion of the single tax on land, Henry George was delighted to discover that a group of French economists, the Physiocrats, had long before proposed the same kind of policy. It was greatly reassuring for George when he perceived that the logic of land rent would imply, for any objective observer, a tax on the value of land. The theory was meaningful, and he had not been the only one to understand its implications. The Physiocrats had also proposed to confiscate all rents from landlords in a position to enjoy what they had not produced.

George recognized that workers and investors have to labor, sacrifice, and make sound decisions to enjoy the fruits of their efforts. But he was convinced that the forces of social progress work against that prospect over time. The solution came as revelation to George that there is no need to confiscate land from those who, often through rather random (if not predatory) processes, had acquired its ownership. This was an important insight for George and for many people anxiously waiting for someone like George to articulate clearly the moral case for *common* ownership of the land that God had given for the well-being and happiness of all humankind.

Given this conviction in an age rich in revolutionary sentiment, it would have been easy to advocate confiscation through the nationalization of land. Marx, Proudhon, and many others had done precisely that, holding that private ownership is theft. Many of George's critics were anxious to pin the socialist label on him, but he only advocated *taxing away* that part of the earnings of landowners that did not come as a reward for effort, investment, or entrepreneurship.

Blaug notes that George aggravated deep fears of revolutionary instincts common to his day with his "widely misunderstood" proposals. He asserts that the misunderstanding was partly because of George's "clumsy exposition, as advocating nationalization of land."[35] In my view, this is a totally undeserved charge. George's policy proposal came into the public view mostly through *Progress and Poverty,* which was widely regarded as a powerful and persuasive work. Few economists of the present or the past could match George's exposition. True, were one to read only through Chapter I of Book VIII, "Private Property in Land Inconsistent with the Best Use of Land," then stop reading precisely at that point (having completed about 70 percent of the book), one might wrongly assume that George was about to announce confiscation of private lands. And when George's policy prescription comes in the next chapter, "How Equal Rights to the Land May be Asserted and Secured," the reader would have to get through a page-and-a-half describing how a society might successfully and profitably abolish "all private titles . . . under such conditions as would sacredly guard the private right to improvements."[36] But he would immediately read on to the plan that George considered best, which was "to abolish all taxation save that upon land values." The narrative is clear, the exposition is flawless. Naturally, careless readers can always draw confusion from clarity, and on that basis, the proposal might have been "widely misunderstood."

A careful reading of George's political activities[37] suggests an alternative reason for the common mistrust of George's real motives. He was heavily engaged in spreading the "cause" of the single taxers, which implied lecture tours in the United States, Europe, and even Australia. There were also publicized political campaigns and activities. His speaking and political efforts (especially those in association with individuals and groups who were not always as clear on their policy objectives or who pursued objectives divergent from those of George) could have been a source of confusion to those who were more inclined to follow newspaper accounts of George's activities than to give his writings serious attention.

In concluding this section, it is important to observe that George's proposal was not a crackpot idea. It was based on the reasoned theories of the Physiocrats, Adam Smith, and other respected classical economists. We will see later that it still commands the respect of most mainstream economists. It was based on the notion of effective principles of taxation that remain part of the discipline of public finance.

George was clearly utopian in his conviction that the single tax on land values would abolish poverty and economic crises. That view rested on the assumption that political actors could and would adopt and implement beneficial economic policies with some consistency, once the truth was made evident to the people. He attributed the cycle largely to the result of speculation in land values, proposing to tax pure ground rent, exempting the returns from improvements on the land. This single tax would put all property on the same basis irrespective of its location. It would dull the incentive to merely hold land speculatively, since it would make doing so taxable.

Marshall on George's Single Tax

Marshall had encountered George in theoretical terms long before he actually participated in their famous debate. He presented lectures on George's *Progress and Poverty* in which he gave a qualified endorsement of a plan that would have all land become the property of the state after the preparatory period of one century. Following that period, the state would sell the land's usufruct for public purposes or for any other contractual purposes the public desired. Marshall seems to have been convinced that the plan would permit countries adopting the scheme "to dispense with the tax-gatherer."[38] This endorsement is certainly enigmatic considering the positions Marshall ultimately assumed in his published works. If actually implemented, such a proposal would likely require a more complete restructuring of property rights than even the seemingly radical George had proposed. Hebert writes that Marshall probably came to think better of the idea, "for he never returned to it."[39]

The process of establishing the microeconomic foundations of factor shares did not invalidate classical views on rent. Had Ricardo failed to clarify what rents are, how could Marshall have developed the more sophisticated notion of quasi-rents? So Marshall should not have taken an uncharitable view of the idea of the single tax based upon the theory of rent, and he did not generally do so. Marshall could afford to concede that while his precocious views of factor pricing were correct, it nevertheless remained true that "the soil receives an income of heat and light, of rain and air, which is independent of man's efforts."[40] Where the land enjoys "advantages of situation," especially common in the case of urban land, such advantages are not the product of any action or merit on the part of the land's immediate owners. Nor did Marshall find that a special tax on such land would directly affect production. "I regard the income derived from them as true rents for all practical purposes," he said.[41]

As concluded earlier, Marshall ultimately took a position on the issue as prompted by his socially conservative inclinations. He felt that his "care for security for property" was a reflection of a deeper concern, namely, a concern for the "security for liberty." A modest portion of the latter might be sacrificed, if really necessary, if somehow it could be guaranteed that doing so would increase by a substantial measure "the security of well-deserving persons against extreme want."[42] Since genuine security had not been achieved to that point, however, he argued that one could not yet preserve such security. And the compelling argument for Marshall was that a "violent confiscation" of genuine rent would so imperil the general security that it should be considered a "blunder from every point of view," for it would assuredly discourage investment and production even more than more moderate taxes applied especially to any kind of profits or quasi-rents.

Since Marshall's time, economists have ceased to debate the issue as to whether a land tax would imply the social justice imputed to it by George and his followers. That concern seems less relevant today with the arrival of the modern state. Whether socially or militarily engaged, it is unlikely that it could generate enough revenues for public purposes from the single tax. The revenue requirements of the modern state have far outgrown those of any earlier era in which the single tax has been discussed.

Heber observes that Marshall was more guarded when writing for the record, but his *Principles* did hold out the prospect of land reform. Finally, in 1909, Marshall supported a national budget of Lloyd George that had proposed the taxing of land values.

Henry George, Francis A. Walker, and the American Economics Establishment

Henry George's broad public recognition was a contrast to his lack of professional reputation in the United States and elsewhere.[43] This section turns to a contemporary of George who certainly did enjoy the honors and recognition of the nascent economics establishment in the United States. The two could never come to an amicable agreement on basic economics conceptions, and Walker was anxious to put the upstart George in his place. It is of interest to note that George still has a discernable influence in American thought, while Walker has left no imprint and is generally unknown to economists today.

Francis Walker (1840–97) was the son of an economist of some stature, Amasa Walker, who saw that Francis received an education at Amherst, where Amasa taught. The outbreak of the Civil War terminated Francis's anticipated legal career. In the conflict, he served with the Army of the Potomac; he was wounded and captured. He returned with the rank of Brigadier General to teach school, turning later to journalism, before taking charge of the Bureau of Statistics in the U.S. Treasury in 1869. He taught political economy and history at Yale's Sheffield Scientific School from 1872 to 1881, when he became president of the Massachusetts Institute of Technology (MIT), a position he retained for the rest of his life.

While at Yale he published *The Wages Question* (1876) and *Money in Its Relation to Trade and Industry* (1879). At MIT he taught economics and published prolifically on economics, statistics, education, and other topics. At the age of 56 he passed away suddenly, and according to Whitaker, "in the full tide of activity and renown."[44] The interaction between George and Walker was representative of that between George and academic economists. George was critical of economics professors as being incapable of serious thought, and he favored a wholesale reconstruction of the discipline. He had a gift for economic reasoning, but Whitaker holds George's real bent to have been ethico-philosophical and his "turn of mind more speculative than analytical."[45]

Both George and Walker had adopted the view that real wages are derived from output, that they are not advances from capital. So they, like others, were able to make early if tenuous steps toward the marginal productivity theory that was to blossom from multiple branches of the profession from the late 1880s.

Walker took pride especially in his analysis of profit. Whereas the British economists had seen the capitalist employer as generating profits representing interest on capital as well as wages for managerial efforts, Walker saw the capitalist as a mere rentier and the entrepreneur acting as the initiator and coordinator of economic activity and receiving profit exclusive of interest. Walker, like George, failed to see factor claims on national income as the resulting aggregate of activity in individual factor markets.

For the sake of comparison, let us consider briefly George's view of population growth. For George, that phenomenon has three distinct effects. First, it increases the demand for land, generating diminishing returns as more extensive and intensive cultivation is undertaken. Second, it increases labor efficiency and greater average product through more complex specialization and division of labor.[46] Finally, it leads to increased agglomeration of population and industry, greatly increasing the value of the land where such agglomeration occurs. Together, these effects make it possible for output per head to rise while population grows and the real wage rate falls. George rejected Malthusian claims that population growth engenders poverty; he placed the blame for poverty on defective human institutions, not nature's niggardliness. He generally treated population growth as exogenous and not in itself a cause for anxiety.

Assuming a constant population, George concludes that "improvement in the arts" will operate in a labor augmenting manner. Such improvement would, in other words, enable the production of the same output with less labor. The view that productivity improvements were simply equivalent to a larger labor force led George to the conclusion that technical progress could not possibly alleviate the land constraint. It simply added to the pressure on natural resources stemming from population growth. George often assumed the worst: "progress" with or without population growth would not improve the lot of the laboring classes. Poverty would deepen as wealth increased, and the result of increased productive power would simply be declining wages. This was unavoidable because land was both monopolized and subject to speculation. Inexorably rising rents and land values would encourage the speculative search for capital gains while speculation withheld land from productive use.

Francis Walker found George's assumption that technical progress is always labor saving, to be implausible. On the contrary, in Walker's view, technical progress is often land saving. And Walker was skeptical about the inevitability of growing shares of national income for rent. The statistical record on rent's share of national income did not justify George's fears.[47] Walker was convinced that, allied with modest population restraint, technical progress could steadily improve living standards for most workers.

Walker was more optimistic about wages and living standards. Endogenous labor efficiency should make an economy of high wages possible. George was certainly in favor of the idea of high wages, since he was convinced that labor efficiency would increase as wages did. High wages would increase self-respect, energy, and hope. This sentiment of Walker and George resonated with Alfred Marshall as well, who declared this proposition more productive of hope than any other he knew.

George had no doubt that tax authorities would be able to isolate pure rent from the returns to improvements on the land, with the possible exception of long-standing improvements such as drainage. He was encouraged with the American practice of distinguishing the site values from those of improvements on the land when taxing real estate. Given George's concern that taxation and protectionism would tend to corrupt public and private morals, it is surprising that he would place his faith in a system that would leave it to administrative authority to determine what share of rental income should be subject to confiscatory taxation.

George believed that the revenue from his single tax would be substantial and that it would grow over time. It would be so large that all other taxes would be unnecessary from a revenue perspective. Their attendant collection costs would be saved, and a surplus would be generated to construct public facilities, to retire the public debt, and to acquire public utilities that would enjoy the capacities of natural monopolies. He obviously had no conception of the exceptional powers of the modern state to spend.

Many were George's supporters from diverse quarters, but the economics establishment and some others reacted to George's proposals with hostility. Francis Walker was described by Whitaker as "apoplectic, denouncing George's program as 'mad and anarchical,' 'truly monstrous,' 'a precious piece of villainy,' and 'steeped in infamy'."[48] This obloquy seems surprising given Walker's grudging acceptance of a long-standing proposal of John Stuart Mill's, that taxation of the "unearned increment" in land values is justified in principle, although impracticable. Mill had hardly been branded as a radical with his argumentation after 1848 that the community as a whole has legitimate claim to natural resources because "no man made the land. It is the original inheritance of the whole species" (Mill [1848] 1965, p. 230). In Europe, continual criticisms were made regarding private property in land, and George was widely read.

He also gave voice to a host of land-nationalizing advocates in America. When, while traveling in England, George had a debate with Marshall, it was the latter who as yet remained largely unknown to the European public.

Although his single tax seemed to some to border on socialism, George could never with fairness be accused of socialist advocacy. His whole system of thought was built upon the tenets of the classical economists. He was as market oriented as Adam Smith and never saw a substantial role for government intervention in market processes. This issue will be addressed with greater completeness when we discuss George's work in the context of modern economics. We conclude here simply with the important observation that his single tax was designed to solve long-standing economic problems and to simplify the government's fiscal and monetary roles.

George was overly optimistic regarding the potential ameliorative effects of the single tax, but he was not mistaken in his economic analysis of the properties of such a tax. As the keystone of his analysis of distribution, the issues of speculation and appropriate taxation of land rents served well to provide a coherent economic view of the world of Henry George.

Appendix

Part I: George's Summary of His Own Theory of Distribution[49]

The three laws of distribution must necessarily correlate with each other. The law of rent is correctly apprehended by the current political economy. As corollaries [we have] the laws of wages and interest, the part of the produce going to the landowner necessarily determining what part shall be left for labor and capital.

Investigation shows that interest must rise and fall with wages, and depends ultimately upon the same thing as rent—the margin of cultivation or point in production where rent begins. With material progress rent everywhere advances [while] wages and interest do not advance, necessitating an examination of the effect of material progress upon the distribution of wealth.

The factors of material progress are increase of population and improvements in the arts. The increasing proportion of the aggregate produce taken in rent reduces wages and interest. Then, assuming no increase of population, improvement in the methods and powers of production tends to produce in a stationary population continuous increase in land values which spring from material progress. Speculation is a most powerful cause of the increase of rent and the crowding down of wages. The necessary result of material progress, land being private property, is, no matter what the increase in population, to force laborers to wages which give but a bare living.

(p. 21)

Private property in land, instead of being necessary to its improvement and use, entails an enormous waste of productive forces. The recognition of the common right to land involves no shock or dispossession, but is to be reached simply by abolishing all taxation save that upon land values.

This inquiry shows that differences in civilization are not due to differences in individuals, but rather to differences in social organization. Progress, always kindled by association, is now, in modern civilization running its course toward anarchy and despotism. This inquiry also identifies the law of social life with the great moral law of justice, and shows how retrogression may be prevented and a grander advance begun.

(p. 23)

Part II: Straightforward Henry George in Geometric Form

According to George, as the "margin of cultivation" declines (i.e., as wages and interest decline), or as the costs of

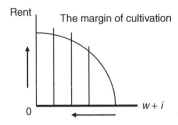

Figure 3A.1   George's Distribution Transformation Curve

agricultural production on the land decline, the share of the economy's total product accruing to rent must increase. This would be seen in a simple Georgian model as movement along a distribution transformation (or factor returns) curve from the right to the left. In Figure 3A.1, three different vertical lines express different possibilities for the margin of cultivation. As we move to a line closer to the origin, we are moving up the curve or seeing rent increase and w (wage) + i (interest) decline. Again, moving to the left causes w and i shares to decline and rent to increase in the process.

Speculation also affects this model by pushing the margin of cultivation line from the right to the left. In George's words, "the speculative advance in land values tends to press the margin of cultivation, or production, beyond its normal limit, thus compelling labor and capital to accept of a smaller return, or (and this is the only way they can resist the tendency) to cease production."[50] Thus, in the course of "progress," wages and interest inevitably and inexorably decline while rent increases.

George held that social progress entails increasing population and land use. There is a functional relationship between the growth of population and land use on the one hand and the growth of rent, the return to the factor land, on the other. That can be shown in our simple model as movement along a "Progress" function, sloping up from the origin to the left in quadrant II, which simply denotes that social progress includes both a growing population and

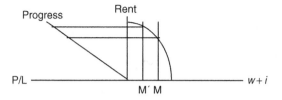

Figure 3A.2   Progress impacts rent, wages and interest

increasing land use (seen as P/L in Figure 3A.2). In sum, as progress occurs, population and land use both increase; rent increases while wages and interest drift downward, as seen by the movement back toward the origin (from right to left) of $w + i$ along the horizontal axis of quadrant I from M to M'.

Social forces automatically push society up the Progress curve, implying larger populations with their accompanying increase in the use of land. This happens despite the fact that more capital-intensive production, promoting greater output through the adoption of new techniques, saves labor. So population/land use, seen in Figure 3A.3 as the P/L axis for quadrants II and III, is a function not only of generally increasing population, but also of the adoption of labor-saving improvements.

The growth of capital-intensive production is reflected in Figure 3A.3 in the Investment curve, expressed as a

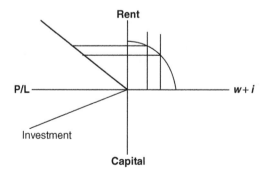

Figure 3A.3   Capital and technology effects in progress

function of growth and development along with increasing population and land use. In George's words, "the effect of inventions and improvements in the productive arts is to save labor—that is, to enable the same result to be secured with less labor, or a greater result with the same labor."[51]

When development and technical change encourage more capital-intensive production, managers will move in that direction. Greater labor-saving investments can be seen as shifting the investment curve downward, as shown in Figure 3A.4. There I becomes I' and later I", showing the increasing use of capital associated with any given point on the progress curve. Movement along the progress line or left along the population/land use axis is a function of increasing population, but also of the adoption of labor-saving improvements. More capital working with labor causes the returns of all factors to increase, that is, it causes the factor returns curve in quadrant I to shift out to the right as shown in Figure 3A.4.

Continuing with the quote above on labor-saving innovations, George writes, "while the primary effect of

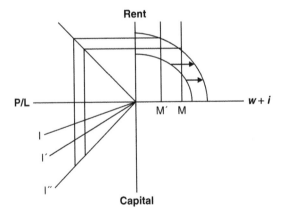

Figure 3A.4 Main elements of distribution theory

labor-saving improvements is to increase the power of labor, the secondary effect is to extend cultivation, and, where this lowers the margin of cultivation, to increase rent."[52] All of the progress moves society to the left on the population/land use axis and causes an increase in the capital stock and in labor-saving innovations as land use increases. But the labor-saving capital causes the factor returns or distribution transformation curve to shift out to the right (permitting workers and capital to enjoy greater factor returns) as shown by the arrows in Figure 3A.4. Being better off, the workers adopt a lifestyle that also uses more land.

The transformation curve's shift out or to the right reflects the increased factor returns in the short run. Unfortunately, in the long run the margin of cultivation declines again as there is a movement *along* the new transformation curve back to the left. Wages and interest are not improved, but as we would expect in a Georgian view of the universe, rent increases. As seen earlier, this is viewed in Figure 3A.4 as a movement in quadrant I from M to M', that is, from the right to the left vertical line (the latter now being the new margin of cultivation produced by investment and labor-saving innovations, resulting in reduced wages and interest along with higher rent). From the higher point on the factor returns curve, the horizontal line over to the progress curve, and the vertical line extending from that point down to the investment curve all reflect greater investments accompanied by increased population and land use, but they also demonstrate the same tendency toward declining wages and interest accompanied by increasing rent. George contends that the long-run tendency is for increasing land use, a tendency which does not exclude land use by successful workers, some of whom apparently become landowners as these developments produce subsequent movement up the progress curve.

Part III: Marshall's Theory of Factor Pricing

Marshall presented his own version of factor pricing in Note XIV of the *Principles*.[53] Let $\alpha_1, \alpha_2, \alpha_3, \ldots, \alpha_n$ represent different kinds of labor to be used in constructing a home. $\beta, \beta', \beta'', \ldots$ represent different kinds of rooms for the home. V will represent total outlays for productive factors, so $V, \beta, \beta', \beta'', \ldots$, are all functions of $\alpha_1, \alpha_2, \alpha_3$. H is basically the housing utility or benefit anticipated from the rooms to be constructed, a function of $\beta, \beta', \beta'', \ldots$ and also of $\alpha_1, \alpha_2, \alpha_3$. For the sake of simplicity, H represents total receipts to be derived from sales of the products factor A will help produce. Marshall seeks to find the marginal investments of each kind of labor for each kind of use with the following expressions.

$$dV = dH\, d\beta = dH\, d\beta' = dH\, d\beta''$$
$$= d\alpha_1\, d\beta\, d\alpha_1\, d\beta'\, d\alpha_1\, d\beta''\, d\alpha_1$$
$$dV = dH d\beta = dH\, d\beta' = dH d\beta''$$
$$= d\alpha_2\, d\beta\, d\alpha_2\, d\beta'\, d\alpha_2\, d\beta''\, d\alpha_2$$

He instructs us that these equations represent a balance of effort and benefit. The real cost to the producer of some small additional amount of labor employed to cut and process timber will be neatly balanced by the benefit accruing to their completed labors. If the principal here decides to pay a carpenter instead of doing the work himself, V will represent not his personal total effort, but his expenditures for the labor employed. In that instance, the rate of pay the carpenters will receive for their additional effort (the agent's marginal demand price for their labor), is given by dV/da; while $dH/d\beta, dH/d\beta'$ are the monetary values to him of the marginal utilities of extra rooms constructed, or his marginal demand prices for them. $d\beta/da$ and $d\beta'/da$ are the marginal efficiencies of carpenters' labor in this project. According to the equations, the demand price for carpenters' labor tends to be equal to the demand price for extra rooms in the home, being multiplied for each room by the marginal efficiency of the carpenters' work in providing that extra accommodation.

Generalizing this statement, the marginal demand price for hired labor is the marginal efficiency of the labor times the marginal demand price for the product. In other words, wages here tend to be equal to the value of the output produced, or the marginal efficiency of a unit of the labor times the value of the additional product generated. Marshall referred to this as the "net product" of the labor employed. He declares this proposition to be very important, containing "within itself the kernel of the demand side of the theory of distribution."[54]

In more current notation, Marshall's outputs $\beta, \beta_1, \ldots, \beta_n = X, X_1, \ldots, X_n$.

His factor inputs $a = f, f_1, \ldots, f_n$

Let $V = C$ (cost), $H = R$ (revenues, receipts, or benefits).

TC, and $X_1, \ldots, X_n$, are functions of $f_1, f_2, \ldots, f_n$.

$H = g(X_1, X_2, X_3)$ and $H = g(f_1, f_2, f_3)$. The equality of marginal returns and costs associated with each input type is expressed thus:

$$MC/df_1 = dC/df_1 = dR/dX_1 \cdot dX_1/df_1 = MR_{x2}/df_2$$
$$= MR_{x3}/df_3 \tag{1}$$

Marshall says that this expression is a balance of effort (input cost) and benefit (utility or potential revenue resulting from the use of an additional unit of an input). We would express this today in a form which Marshall would have understood immediately. For the competitive case, the value of the marginal product of input a will tend to an equality with the wage of input a. More generally, the value of the marginal product of any input will be equal to the price (cost) of that input.

As we saw above, the value of the marginal product of input a is VMP_a (the price of X times the marginal product of input a, MP_a). The firm's optimization is achieved by setting $VMP_a = w_a$. Rewriting, $p_x = w_a/MP_a$, or $1/p_x = MP_a/p_a$ or MP_a/w_a. For imperfectly competitive industries, the marginal revenue product, MRP_a is defined as the marginal revenue of the output, MR_x, times the marginal product of input a, so that $MRP_a = MR_x(MP_a)$. The only difference between the competitive and imperfectly competitive cases being the use of p_x in competition (which is to be equated to marginal cost for an optimization of net revenue) and MR_x in imperfect competition (which is lower than p_x and in this case is equated to marginal cost in the stead of the price).

In Marshall's equation (1), the expression $dR/dX_1 \cdot dX_1/df_1$ combines two derivatives, both the increase of revenues as output increases at the margin and the increase of output as the use of factor input 1 is increased at the margin. The first expression represents marginal revenue and the second expression represents marginal physical product. So Marshall equates the marginal cost of hiring input 1 to the marginal revenue product of that input. These are very contemporary expressions of economic principles.

Note that the inputs or factors of production are interchangeable. The market for each one operates rather independently of the markets of other inputs. Land adds to production as do other inputs and is not treated differently from them. The demand for an input is a derived demand, derived from the demand for the product which that input helps produce. In short, the Marshallian theory has merely been tweaked, that is, it has been clothed in modern notation and presented in more restrictive form to characterize the value to a firm of a factor's output as marginal productivity times the market price (or in cases of imperfect competition, the marginal revenue). This should help the reader see the nature of the Marshallian contribution and view it as an extension of the classical theory.

CHAPTER 4

Henry George on Free Trade and Protection

Introduction

George recognized the importance of the question of international trade for the study of economics. He took a strong position on the issue of free trade early in his career and defended it vigorously. Strong arguments for free trade and an attack on protectionism were the main thrust of his book *Protection or Free Trade: An Examination of the Tariff Question, with Especial Regard to the Interests of Labor,* published in 1886. This publication represents an important contribution to economics, for the profession has informally adopted and long advocated free trade on the basis of argumentation by great economists such as Adam Smith, David Ricardo, and many others in the mainstream, including, of course, Henry George.

George's book goes beyond a mere refutation of the basic tenets of protectionism, invoking some arguments that remain relevant, although often forgotten in our time. George places the free trade argument in a contemporaneous context, viewing protectionism as a form of taxation on the working man, but also as an integral part of the economic and social establishment of his time. Free trade advocacy was, for George, only a part of the complex of issues relating to the *Progress and Poverty* of his time and to the issues of private property in and the monopolization of land.

For George, the tariffs of his day were a part of a system of taxation he would not have accepted as a "second best" system of taxation. He is widely known for having advocated a land tax, an *impot unique,* which he was convinced would solve many social problems. For him, free trade meant the elimination of the tariff (a foreign trade tax vastly inferior to the single tax), but also of every other restraint on trade both domestic and foreign.

But George's general economic views, a rather orthodox concatenation of classical doctrines, have already been addressed. The effort here will be to consider his contributions to the general theory of international economics, doctrine he considered well established and relatively complete. Using that doctrine, and improving upon it, George felt that he had "stripped the vexed tariff question of its greatest difficulties, and . . . cleared the way for the settlement of a dispute which otherwise might go on interminably."[1]

Through the entire work, George insists that workers are not convinced by academic arguments for free trade and he gives some cogent reasons why they will never accept free trade arguments and why their opposition dooms them. Today, one might be more inclined to hope that a coalition of consumers and uncaptured politicians might ultimately confront the labor/political interests that have imposed heavy taxes on consumers to secure a favored position for the smaller segment of the polity claiming legislative protection. Perhaps this perspective did occur to George; he may have considered labor and consumers as synonymous groups.

George begins the work that will be the basis of our discussion by describing a "great bull . . . tethered by a ring in his nose," outside his office window. This creature he deemed to be "no unfit emblem of the working masses: Grazing round and round he has wound his rope about the stake until now he stands a close prisoner." A want of understanding and political impotency "must continue until the masses, or at least that sprinkling of more thoughtful men who are the file-leaders of popular opinion, shall give such heed to larger questions as will enable them to agree on the path reform should take." This chapter addresses George's views on reform for the foreign trade of his country.

The following sections will review, first, George's basic theoretical views on trade, including both his economic case for free trade and his ethical case. Several fundamental arguments going beyond the traditional specialization and efficiency tenets in favor of free trade are the subject of the next section. The tariff, as a form of taxation, and its impact as an indirect tax, is considered. A subsequent section is devoted to some quite "modern" trade issues in George's writings; then some of the practical problems associated with tariffs are reviewed from his perspective. George's view of U.S. tariff history and his belief that the logic of trade theory could not be accepted by the laboring classes are addressed in a final section. The implications of their situation suggested to him that reforms designed merely to achieve free trade would remain insufficient. To overcome the poverty linked with the progress he observed, more extensive reforms, such as those he had long advocated, would have to be undertaken.

Why Free Trade?

George's Economic Case for Free Trade

George attacks head-on the argument that protection leads to great opportunities and high wages for labor. He denies that through trade protection society can assure "the greatest comfort, the widest diffusion of knowledge, the purest morals and the truest patriotism" for the most "healthy, happy, enlightened and virtuous"[2] people. According to him, the advocates of protection are prepared to make large expenditures to propagate their doctrines and are thus in a position to "exert great influence upon the organs of public opinion."[3] In contrast, the advocates of free trade can bestow no special advantage on any particular interest; moreover, social benefits or damage widely shared "are not felt so intensely as those which affect them specially."[4]

George sees free trade as that which occurs naturally in the absence of artificial restrictions. It was protectionism rather than free trade that had to be invented, something that had occurred in Great Britain long before there was any United States. The intellectual reaction against it had occurred in France under Quesnay and other French *économistes,* who were predecessors and in many things teachers of Adam Smith. George admired them because they advocated not only the elimination of protective duties, but of all duties whatsoever, all of which were to be replaced by a single tax on land.

To argue that labor requires protection is to degrade the laborer to the position of a dependent, George believed.[5] The common man has been "benefited" by the protection of various kinds of tyrannies—monarchy, aristocracy, and other privileged leadership groups. And George suspected that contemporary protectionists were as little interested in the well-being of the worker as others offering protection in the past.

George appeals to reason by explaining how he came to doubt the protectionists, beginning with his original exposure to the doctrine by an "able man"[6] urging that American industries receive protection from the competition of foreign producers. He advocated manufacturing on the basis of our own raw materials, allowing no imports that could be produced in the country. If that general proposition is beneficial for one country, George reasoned, it must be valid as well for every other. If autarky is best, it must be an applicable principle not only for nations, but for regions within countries, which should likewise impose tariffs on the imports from other regions. And if the principle is true that people should obtain nothing abroad that they can make themselves, it should apply to the family as well. This, George said, led him to weigh arguments very carefully that he had previously accepted without critical evaluation.[7] Seeing protection in this light led George to conclude that free trade is the appropriate policy. Complete autarky would leave isolated individuals completely independent and completely impoverished just as it leaves nations underdeveloped economically.

Free Trade as an Optimal Policy: Add Transactions, Transportation, Tariffs

In the standard university course on international economics, the simple logic of free trade abstracts from such complications as transportation costs and institutional trade barriers, which must be incorporated later. The theory is based on a comparison of labor costs and initially ignores other factors of production. George's analysis is in the spirit of the contemporary, basic trade course. Let us look briefly at the extension of his analysis with a more comprehensive evaluation of autarky versus trade, which remains at the heart of the public debate on protection.

To production cost (PC), which may be assumed to be just labor, or realistically more complex, must be added transactions costs (TrC), which include all the normal ones—information and marketing costs, negotiations costs, et cetera. Transport costs (TC) must be added as well. These are considered to be 0 for a firm that operates strictly locally, since they will not be significant enough to affect the cost level that makes specialization profitable. They will be 1 and can also be prohibitively high for interregional transport.

The nub of the argument is that specialization reduces cost, opening up the necessity to distribute specialized production and enjoy trade's benefits. We begin with small units (SU) that include family-based production. If the cost price of potential small unit production, $CPsu, = PC + TC + TrC < MP$, the local market price, a small unit will (1) produce and sell locally and (2) organize itself into a firm, since the small unit's cost price is less than that of the local market. (The decision becomes, "don't buy, make.")

The addition of TrC and TC can offset or nullify the prospective benefits of specialization. If they do not, if a firm is organized and if sales start to occur beyond the local area, we have evidence of the benefits of specialization. The motivation to find and develop products that enable a firm to be organized and begin to function on an interregional basis, we expect to be constant and strong. It is, of course, the profit motive that gives robustness to the system.

Natural spatial barriers impose TC, which have declined through time but remain too great to assume away, as we initially do in explicating the benefits of comparative advantage. Of these, contemporary trucking and rail modes for national or regional transport services are far more effective and low cost than those of George's time.[8] International trade is generally more concerned with maritime and air transportation, which have likewise declined greatly over the long term (sometimes being referred to as an "enabling factor" in trade), even enough to be assumed away in trade theory discussions.[9] It should be noted, of course, that aggregate international *ad valorem* TC have not decreased over the last three decades for many countries and products. What would happen if today we could somehow achieve a 20 percent reduction in all transport margins (the share of TC in the total PC of traded goods)? It is estimated[10] that the effect would nearly be equivalent to a complete elimination of the world's remaining trade barriers. Achieving such liberalization would assure welfare gains, in other words, of the same magnitude as a reduction in TC by 20 percent. Doing so would enhance U.S. household incomes by about $9 billion.

In an energy crisis, however, we have to ask whether long-term TC will not rise significantly on the wings of higher fuel prices. The time might be rapidly approaching in which less abundant oil will no longer permit the assumption of zero TC. When we consider interregional and global trade regimes, TC for some goods could be sufficiently high that the formation of regional trading arrangements may be superior to global free trade. Moving from local to regional trade, firms presumed to have a comparative advantage will engage in trade if their cost price is less than the market price elsewhere within the same region, defined as an area of feasible TC and open trade borders.

But at this point we encounter an additional, new form of TC, a synthetic TrC that Henry George would have thought of as being conspiratorial. It consists of the imposition of taxes on competitive products produced beyond the local region and imported. For George, additional costs of this *genre* included not only tariffs, but the transactions costs of intricate customs procedures, inadequate implementation of information and communications technologies, insurance payments, and other international financial requirements.

The specific purpose of tariffs, quotas, voluntary export restraints, et cetera, is to restore the higher-cost, less-appealing domestic product to ostensible competitiveness. These policy tools represent a conspiracy between high-cost local producers and political agents acting against their own citizens. Their results are higher prices and lower quality products and can potentially reduce the country's standard of living significantly. Politicians will not find their conspiratorial activities an impediment to the retention of power, since taxpayers *cum* voters have no objection to high taxes if revenues are extracted in small bites with the whole process remaining opaque. Nor do the politicians object to the tax revenues, although they have been known in one recent case even to cede such revenues back to the protected local producers (as under the infamous Bird Amendment in the United States).

Where to the transactions costs (TrC) are added the synthetic (or State) transactions costs, STrC, representing trade barriers, foreign competition can be significantly reduced and a market that would otherwise be a regional market becomes a local market. The cost price for regional (international) trade can now be expressed as:

$$CP = PC + TC + TrC + STrC < MP_{regional}$$

If it is less than the market price of another country or targeted trade region, a firm will (1) open up trade with that region and (2) become (in post-Georgian parlance) a multinational corporation (MNC), which may include establishing a subsidiary firm or plant in the targeted region. With the cost price equation, we can quickly glance over the cost elements and make some inferences about what the cost impact will be if we establish a production unit in the targeted region rather than produce domestically and export to that region. We observe that $CP = PC$ (including fixed costs we could sink in establishing a plant through a joint venture in the target country) + TC (transport costs, which may be eliminated if the firm begins to produce in the targeted country or region) + TrC (which may be smaller if the firm establishes a production unit in the targeted region) + STrC (which may be avoided if the regional firm doesn't export its products but produces them within the targeted region). So if the comparative advantage of the exporting firm can be retained in a new location, the cost price may be susceptible to greater reduction by relocating production to the foreign country.

If the targeted country has trade barriers in place to avoid competition, its tariff rates may be high enough to put the cost price of the producer above the price of domestic production in that country. Or, if the host state is determined that competition is to be avoided, it is not likely that a foreign firm will be permitted to begin production within its borders.

To conclude this section, it is worth mentioning that given the cost function, the optimal level of outputs for the exporting firm can be calculated in a straightforward manner.[11] The economic case shows it to be in the self-interest of the exporting firm and the consumers in the targeted area to trade at the lower price level of the exporting country. The exporting firm can maximize profit and sell at a price and volume that will provide consumers with greater benefits than were available in the absence of trade. The price will remain lower than the regional price in the targeted area so long as synthetic transactions costs (in the form of trade barriers), are not introduced and other costs (transport and normal transactions costs) do not impose a barrier greater than the benefits of specialization.

This completes the economic case for free trade, but George was also interested in the ethical case.

George's Ethical Case for Free Trade

In George's view, both religion and human experience demonstrate that the highest good can be achieved only in seeking good for others. He sees no conflict between the self-interest that motivates trade and the welfare interests of the potential buyers. George did not see the convergence of seller and importer interests as a matter of chance or good fortune. He saw the true interests of men as being harmonious rather than antagonistic. He argued that "prosperity is the daughter of good will and peace and that want and destruction follow enmity and strife."[12] In opposition to this, the advocates of protection of George's day, who would not differ from those of our own time, saw trade as a zero-sum game, as "the opposition of national interests" implying "the gain of one people is the loss of others." In George's view, attempting to get the advantage over potential trading partners before they can take advantage of you makes rivals of nations, inculcating a "warfare of restrictions and prohibitions and searchings and seizures, which differs in weapons, but not in spirit, from that warfare which sinks ships and burns cities."[13]

Reminding us of the swords, plowshares, and pruning hooks of Isaiah, George could not imagine peace and cooperation coming in the face of hostile tariffs. Regardless of a man's religious (or irreligious) persuasion, no rational observer can avoid seeing the want and suffering that inevitably flow from selfishness. In any community, George wrote, "the golden rule which teaches us to regard the interests of others as carefully as our own would bring not only peace but plenty."[14]

Additional Arguments against Protection

Protection versus War Blockades

George compared protective tariffs to another application of state power, that is, to blockading squadrons imposed on an enemy country in times of war. He insisted that tariffs are no less an application of national force and have the same objective of preventing trade. Blockading squadrons are used to prevent an enemy from being able to participate in trade for products that may be needed, in part, to conduct the national defense. They are only different from tariffs in that they are a means to prevent enemies (rather than fellow citizens) from trading; protective tariffs, in contrast, are a means of preventing a nation's own people from trading. George makes the striking point that protection does to a nation in time of peace "what enemies seek to do to us in time of war."[15]

Protectionism as "Restrictionism"

Advocates of protection promote systems of "restriction" that lack the essential qualities of real protection. George pointed out that such restrictions do not defend people against external hazards or enemies, but they protect people from doing what they themselves want to do. Such "protection," George reminded, is not that of a superior intelligence, "for human wit has not yet been able to devise any scheme by which any intelligence can be secured in a Parliament or Congress superior to that of the people it represents."[16]

Homo sapien as a Trade Creature

Trade among peoples is as natural, according to George, as the circulation of blood. The species is by nature a trading animal, driven to trade by constant innate desires. We have been placed in a world in which everything demonstrates how we were intended to trade, and how through that activity we discover the possibility of social advance. George asserts: "Without trade man would be a savage."[17] In that state of society in which each family "raises its own food, builds its own house, makes its own clothes and manufactures its own tools, no one can have more than the barest necessaries of life, and every local failure of crops must bring famine."[18] Such families will enjoy independence, but they will live in poverty and ignorance, remaining powerless against the wiles and vicissitudes of nature.

Civilization a Function of Trade

George's experience had convinced him that wealth first began to accumulate and civilization began to take root as a response to the possibilities of commercial trade. The great cities of today are yesterday's trading venues, located on trade routes—accessible harbors, heavily traveled highways, and the shores of navigable rivers. It was in such cities that the arts and sciences began to develop. Trade becomes free and extensive as roads become passable and are extended, navigation is improved, and the rule of law replaces pirates, robbers, and local warfare. As this occurs, wealth increases and civilization is extended. Great labor-saving inventions develop with and facilitate trade, which has always tended to extinguish war, eradicate prejudice, and diffuse knowledge. Trade causes the spread of productive agriculture and horticulture as well as useful arts and technologies. Trade carries things of worth all over the world, enabling participants to obtain products and benefit from "the observations, discoveries and inventions of men in other places."[19] George aptly makes an observation that should (but probably will not) bring peace to those who fear and oppose the "globalization" of the present day: "The appointed condition of human progress is evidently that men shall come into closer relations and become more and more dependent upon each other."[20]

The Tariff as a Form of Indirect Tax

Having banished the misconception that tariffs are useful as a means of protecting domestic industry, George contends that the only justification for a tariff is its capacity to raise revenue. So one should understand the implications of the fact that trade duties are a form of indirect tax. The question for George becomes whether indirect taxation is an appropriate means for raising revenue for the state.

It should come as no surprise, especially to the specialist who will have observed long ago that governments nearly always choose to implement the wrong kinds of taxes, that there are some serious problems with indirect taxation. First, this kind of tax is certainly not an example of one that features ease of collection. Direct taxes, says George, such as the property tax and the inheritance tax, can readily generate considerable revenue with low collection costs. Indirect taxes, by contrast, if they can generate any significant revenue at all, do so only with the employment of "large and expensive staffs of officials and the enforcement of vexatious and injurious regulations."[21] But even after they are in place and the accompanying prohibitions, warnings, monitoring and searches, restrictions, et cetera, people generally manage to evade indirect taxes on commodities, sometimes by bribing officials and sometimes by simple stealth. Although such dishonesty is costly to maintain, eluding the vigilance of the customs bureaucracy will cost less than paying the taxes.

In the long run, of course, all such costs ultimately fall on consumers as the increased costs are passed on in the form of higher prices. But such taxation is extremely wasteful and inefficient, since it extracts from consumers much more than the government obtains. (In modern parlance this observation takes the form of the statement "customs revenues reduce consumer surplus by a much smaller amount than the total losses accruing to trade restrictions.") An even more important objection George had to indirect taxation was that when imposed on commodities used widely (the only commodities from which such taxes can generate significant revenues), its impact is far heavier on and more damaging to the poor than to affluent buyers.[22] It is unfortunate, George observes, that the incidence of this kind of tax affects individuals "not according to what they have, but according to what they consume, it is heaviest on those whose consumption is largest in proportion to their means."[23]

George saw in indirect taxation the omnipresent tendency to load heavier taxes on inexpensive items of common use than on the more costly articles used only by the rich. But this was not necessarily seen as conspiratorial, since the necessities of indirect taxation explain it. Articles commonly consumed offer the potential of a wider revenue base than the smaller consumption of more costly articles. Moreover, taxes imposed on the items of common usage cannot be so easily evaded.

The Benefits of Indirect Taxation

But the use of taxes that weigh heavily on the poor was not seen by George as being strictly a matter of convenience of implementation. The rich and the powerful have inordinate influence under all types of government and also in forming public opinion, while the poor are always essentially without voice. Indirect taxes are also collected, especially from the poor, in such insidious ways that they do not realize the loss. Such taxes thus permit the collection of the largest revenues with the least remonstrance from the general public against the sums collected or against the expenditures they enable. George considered this to be the principal reason governments have relied so extensively on indirect taxation.

Indirect Tax and Industrial Concentration

George was convinced that indirect taxation tends to promote industrial concentration. The notion deserves direct quotation:

> Indirect taxes add to the price of goods not only the tax itself but also the profit upon the tax. If on goods costing a dollar a manufacturer or merchant has paid fifty cents in taxation, he will now expect profit on a dollar and fifty cents instead of upon a dollar... The need of larger capital for dealing in goods that have been enhanced in cost by taxation, the restrictions imposed on trade to secure the collection of the tax, and the better opportunities which those who do business on a large scale have of managing the payment or evading the tax, tend to concentrate business, and, by checking competition, to permit large profits, which must ultimately be paid by consumers.[24]

For George, monopoly was a danger imminently present in the developing economy of the United States in the nineteenth century. Nevertheless, monopoly, land speculation, and inept governmental policies were not symptomatic of general systemic failure as were capitalist phenomena for Marx. George believed firmly in reform and the possibility of amelioration of social problems through policy measures. He was convinced that he had presented in *Progress and Poverty* the solution to the problems that condemned many to poverty in the midst of general social progress. Others could also be enlightened through the processes of education (not synonymous, of course, with formal higher education). In the meantime, Congress was surrounded by lobbyists clamoring for legislation to promote special interests. Issues of extreme importance were often ignored in the struggle "for the spoils of taxation." George's optimism came out in his conclusion that "under such a system of taxation our government is not far more corrupt than it is, is the strongest proof of the essential goodness of republican institutions."[25]

In conclusion, George did not deny that indirect taxes sometimes serve purposes other than raising revenue. When that was all they did, however, he found them worthy of condemnation. Their social costs far exceeded their yield, they burdened those least able to pay them "with the greatest weight," they represented a corruptive influence, and they actually reduced the control the citizens had over their government.

Bounties versus Tariffs

Like some more modern economists, Henry George saw bounties or subsidies to inefficient or neophyte producers as being superior to tariff protection. It seems even more superior with increases in the number of industries the government desires to protect. Promoting industrial development through a subsidy does not have a negative impact on other industries, except for any addition to the general level of taxation that also applies to business. When one industry is "encouraged," however, by a tariff, all other industries dependent on that product as an input of production suffer the directly injurious effects of the higher costs. George felt constrained to admit that providing subsidies had historically been both tainted with fraud and corruption and lacking in effect, just as they had been with the large subsidies granted to the railroads. But, said he, "these evils are inseparable from any method of 'encouragement,' and attach to the protective more than to the bounty system." George's inference that protection is an inferior policy was in part due to the fact that protective effects are not often transparent. "If protection has been preferred to bounties it is not that it is a better means of encouragement, but for the same reason that indirect has been preferred to direct taxation—because the people do not so readily realize what is being done."[26]

"Modern" International Trade Issues Addressed by Henry George

The author will hopefully be forgiven for injecting at this point a personal comment regarding George's contribution on modern trade issues. A lot of time has gone by since George wrote, and many brilliant minds have seen fit to make important comments and contributions on international trade issues. We will review some of these momentarily. When I went back to review Henry George's work on trade I was surprised at the number of issues he addressed that I thought had not appeared on the scene until later or much later. These are issues that gave scholars like Heckscher, Ohlin, and Paul Samuelson, and the authors who worked with them, a good deal of scholarly fame along with Nobel Prizes in economics. As will be seen, these more modern scholars worked out their theories and theorems with rigor and mathematics. On the basis of their work's quality, some of those involved would doubtless have also won the Nobel. But the prize is not given posthumously and they would have had to live very long lives to have won it. Henry George preceded them by many years, but was already aware of issues that they would address much later. Moreover, using the old classical economics, George thought carefully and systematically about the same issues and generally came very early to the correct conclusions as we shall see. With these issues, we see once again how George was able to extend beyond the classical foundations and produce sound, sometimes brilliant results. He was simply a great scholar and probably the best of those produced by early, postbellum America in economics.

Fair Trade

It is interesting to learn that the seemingly contemporary issue of "fair trade" has been around for some time. That George wrote about it is no significant credit to him, since he was just reporting on what he observed. And that was that British protectionists had recently assumed the title "fair traders." The point they wished to make was that free trade may essentially be reasonable, but as long as other nations retain protective tariffs, the British should do likewise in self-defense. Countries that refuse to admit British exports duty free should have to pay duty to access the British market.[27] Since that time, fair traders have tended to argue that since nobody really supports free trade, we should all oppose it as "fair traders."

The "Optimal Tariff"

George addressed the idea that tariffs are sometimes advantageous because their burden falls on the producers of imported goods, which would mean that optimal tariffs are taxes paid by foreigners. If George had lived in our day, he might have become a Nobel laureate for this insight, especially since it was not his only one.

George believed that under certain circumstances foreign monopolists might actually pay the tariffs for the importers of their products. Contemporary theory recognizes that the tariff costs of an imported commodity produced by a "closely controlled foreign monopoly" may in some instances accrue either in whole or in part to the foreign producer. The instances referred to, George failed to note, have to be those in which the importing countries have monopsonistic power. That is to say that they must be large countries representative of an important fraction of the exporter's total market.

George theorized that a foreign firm enjoys a monopoly in some export commodity, permitting it to fix the price at the level it believes will produce maximum net revenues. But the imposition of a significant import duty raises the sales price to an extent that would substantially curtail consumption in the import market. The exporting firm, anxious to avoid seeing its share of this important market decline substantially, would even be willing to reduce its price to retain sales. In doing so, it would achieve less profit while the tariff revenues continue to come in. It is in effect simply paying the tax. George wrote that such a firm may "prefer to reduce their profit on what they sell to this country rather than have the sale diminished by the addition of the duty to the price. In such case the duty will fall upon them."[28]

But this is a rare circumstance, George admitted. Such cases, he was convinced, were insignificant with regard to their contributions to national revenue. But the possibility is of interest since it represents "rare exceptions to the general rule that the ability to tax ends with the territorial limits of the taxing power."[29] Unfortunately, the possibility of exceptional cases in which import duties may in part or in whole fall on foreign producers instead of domestic consumers, has in it, even for those who would gladly tax "foreigners," no shadow of a recommendation for protection. The cases in which an import duty falls on foreign producers are cases that offer no encouragement to home producers. An import duty can only fall on foreign producers when its payment does not increase the domestic price; the only possible way in which an import duty can encourage home producers is by adding to price. But George failed to make the observation that revenue-hungry advocates of such tariffs should be aware that the potential retaliation of erstwhile trade partners could not only end the effectiveness of the optimal tariff, but the profitable trade interaction of the two nations involved as well.

George, Stolper, and Samuelson: Trade and Factor Returns

Well after George's time, Stolper and Samuelson carried the reasoning of Ricardo, Heckscher, and Ohlin to its apparent conclusion. They observed that specialization and trade will bring higher returns to factors of production used intensively and that factors used less intensively, providing less assistance in the pursuit of specialization's cornucopian benefits, would experience a decline in their returns. Assuming pure competition (the absence of pure profits) in trading industries, Samuelson and Stolper reasoned and mathematically demonstrated that an increase in a good's price (as a result, say, of the opening of trade and the addition of foreign demand to that of domestic demand for a product of comparative advantage) will result in an increase in the price of the factor used intensively in that industry and a decrease in the price of the other factor. The mathematical derivation[30] elegantly demonstrates the soundness of simple logic. When trade opens and specialization is pursued, the commodity a country produces will be suggested by its comparative advantage. That commodity will be produced in greater amounts as its price rises due to the addition of foreign demands to that of the home country. A country like the United States in the mid-nineteenth century will have a comparative advantage in the commodity wheat, which will be produced so that its price will be equal to its marginal cost, which will be the sum of the increased total outlays for land and the increased total outlays for labor.

Martin has addressed George's theories in their historical context.[31] George fought against tariffs especially through the administrations of Garfield, who with the Republicans of his time successfully pushed for increases in protection, and Cleveland, who with the Democrats was ineffective in staving off the demands for greater protection. In the optimism of the early Cleveland presidency, George wrote his book and some articles on trade correctly analyzing the American situation decades in advance of the appearance of the Stolper-Samuelson theorem.

The Stolper-Samuelson theorem predicts that free trade will increase the prices of the relatively abundant factors of production relative to the scarce ones. If the scarce factors are, on the contrary, protected, they will benefit with higher returns. Those who pay the price of "protection" are the owners of the relatively abundant, relatively inexpensive factors. George recognized and discussed the relative abundance of the factors in the United States as compared with England.[32] He expected that protectionism would reverse the movement in relative factor prices that trade would promote, reducing the demand for the relatively abundant factor, labor, and increasing the demand for and returns to capital and land, just as the modern theory predicts.

George on Tariffs, Goods and Labor Markets

Let us begin our more detailed discussion with the reminder that George had rejected the wages fund theory with the suggestion that laborers created their own wages as they labored.[33] Harrison discusses George's notion of a free farmer agreeing to switch to wage labor only if it would bring him an income at least equal to what he could earn at the margin of cultivation applying his labor to the land without paying rent. On the other side of the transaction, employers facing competition would offer wages no higher than those sufficient to attract labor away from self-employment. Thus, wages depend upon the margin of production, the largest possible output labor can obtain without the payment of rent. But where employment opportunities are monopolized, the competition of workers may force wages down to the minimum at which labor can reproduce itself. Harrison correctly asserts that this reasoning anticipated the marginalist revolution and the neoclassical work of Alfred Marshall.[34]

George believed that tariffs affected prices in commodity markets but not in labor markets. On encountering George's view that "the aim of protection is to lessen competition in the selling of commodities, not in the selling of labor" and that a tariff on commodities can in no case "benefit those who have labor, not commodities, to sell,"[35] one is likely to gain the impression that George intellectually separated labor and commodity markets, seeing no interaction between them of the type that is at the base of the Stolper-Samuelson effect.

In George's view, protection was not considered by the industrial "beneficiaries" of such policies as obliging them to share their benefits with labor. Tariffs protect employers in commodity markets, but leave free trade conditions in the labor market. So even in "protected industries" labor would still be under the necessity of having to organize. But the supposition that George saw no natural link between those markets would be superficial. He was observing different conditions that were prevalent in his time and he was anxious to explain them.

Those very industrialists who "profess anxiety to protect American labor by raising the price of what they themselves have to sell," he wrote, buy labor "as cheap as they can and fiercely oppose any combination of workmen to raise wages." They purchase their labor, in other words, *in a purely competitive labor market at market-clearing prices.*[36] So the competitive conditions stipulated in the Stolper-Samuelson theorem apply to George's labor markets.

He insisted that any assertion that protective policies would raise wages had to rely on two assumptions: "(1) that increase in the profits of employers means increase in the wages of their workmen; and (2) that increase of wages in the protected occupations involves increase of wages in all occupations."[37] George bluntly affirms that even to state such assumptions is to demonstrate their absurdity. "Is there anyone," he asks, "who really supposes that because an employer makes larger profits he therefore pays higher wages?"[38] Buyers, he reminded us, pay what they must, not what they can, keeping motives of benevolence for other than business activities. Higher, protected profits will certainly not be shared with the working people.

Envisioning a competitive labor market with a price reflecting competitive conditions, with the vocabulary of our own day George would have said that labor will receive the value of their marginal product. In the neoclassical model, organized workers could receive higher wages through bilateral bargaining processes in an imperfectly competitive market offering the possibility of monopsonistic profits. In George's terms: "No matter how much a protective duty may increase the profits of employers, it will have no effect in raising wages unless it so acts upon competition as to give workmen power to compel an increase of wages."[39]

George may well have envisioned wages quite instinctively as the product of the price of a good (reflecting its demand) and the marginal productivity of the laborer. At the same time, he saw industrial labor as generally unskilled and in very abundant supply as more and more workers streamed from farm to nascent factory. He wrote:

> As for the great mass of those engaged in the protected industries, their labor can hardly be called skilled. Much

of it can be performed by ordinary unskilled laborers, and much of it does not need even the physical strength of the adult man, but consists of the mere tending of machinery, or of manipulations which can be learned by boys and girls in a few weeks, a few days, or even a few hours. As to all this labor, which constitutes by far the greater part of the labor required in the industries we most carefully protect, any temporary effect which a tariff might have to increase wages in the way pointed out would be so quickly lost that it could hardly be said to come into operation. For an increase in the wages of such occupations would at once be counteracted by the flow of labor from other occupations. And it must be remembered that the effect of "encouraging" any industry by taxation is necessarily to discourage other industries, and thus to force labor into the protected industries by driving it out of others.[40]

George complained vituperatively that wages in protected industries were, "if anything, lower than in the unprotected industries." His empirical assertion remained untested that although protected industries in the United States employed only about a twentieth of the total labor force, "there occur in them more strikes, more lockouts, more attempts to reduce wages, than in all other industries." He concluded that "all the forms and evidences of the oppression and degradation of labor" were "throughout the country, characteristic of the protected industries."[41]

It was the victory of land and land ownership that George held responsible for the difficult circumstances of labor. We find in civilized countries, George observed, a large class of laborers who, denied any right to the ownership and use of the elements (land and primary resources) required to market their labor power, must either pay rent for "a part of the produce of their labor, or take in wages less than their labor yields."[42] Landholders, in George's view, were "held to be the absolute owners of the material universe, while other men cannot use it without paying tribute." The tendency of such ownership is to "destroy independence, to dispense with skill and convert the artisan into a 'hand,' to concentrate all business and make it harder for an employee to become his own employer, and to compel women and children to injurious and stunting toil."[43]

According to George, workers knew by their bitter experience that an increase in general wealth did not imply any amelioration in their own condition. While labor in the United States had watched the general wealth of the country increase dramatically and the fortunes of the rich grow in like manner, it had not become the slightest bit easier for workers to get a living.

The workers did not understand, unfortunately, what political economy demonstrated: while many products steadily fell in value, there was a steady increase in the value of land. He wrote:

> Inventions and discoveries that increase the productive power of labor lessen the value of the things that require labor for their production, but increase the value of land, since they increase the amount that labor can be compelled to give for its use. And so, where land is fully appropriated as private property no increase in the production of wealth, no economy in its use, can give the mere laborer more than the wages of the slave. If wealth rained down from heaven or welled up from the depths of the earth it could not enrich the laborer. It could merely increase the value of land.[44]

And how did capital fit into this scheme? For George, it was the product of land and labor, the primary factors of production. The capitalist was simply an "intermediary between the landlord and the laborer." Laborers should not see capital as their oppressor. What appears on the surface to be oppression by capital is actually just the result of the "helplessness to which labor is reduced by being denied all right to the use of land."

Capital would have no power to compel men to sell their labor for subsistence wages if they were granted "free access

to nature." Moreover, "capitalistic monopolies" could succeed in appropriating labor's wages only to the extent that
landownership did not confiscate them first. Whether social
organization were simple or complex, whether the interme-
diaries between the owners of land and the workers were few
or many, because the appropriation of land made it the property of a specific group of landholders, "there must exist a
class, the laborers of ordinary ability and skill, who can never
hope to get more than a bare living for the hardest toil, and
who are constantly in danger of failure to get even that."[45]

George on Factor Use in a Neoclassical Framework

Let us see how well this doctrine fits into a neoclassical
framework with the appropriate two commodity world of
wheat and cloth. With the specification of competitive conditions in labor markets and imperfect competition in land
markets, it is not necessary to be concerned with whether
land is the intensive or abundant factor in the production
of wheat (the Georgian literature tends to argue, as we saw,
that George perceived this not to be the case).

We posit the opening of trade and specialization in wheat
as the appropriate course for the United States with the production of cloth as the comparative advantage of our trade
partner, Britain. George was willing to assume the competitive market for labor mentioned earlier, but parted with
Samuelson and Stolper by insisting that the market for land
was characterized by imperfect competition. The demand
for land, given by the marginal revenue product of land,
$\text{MRP}_b = \text{MP}_b(\text{MR}w)$, is equal to the marginal product
of land times the marginal revenue for wheat. From the
competitive labor market, the demand for farm labor would
be the value of the marginal product of labor, $\text{VMP}_a = \text{MP}_a(p_w)$, which is equal to the marginal product of labor
times the price of wheat. As usual, the VMP_a is equal to
the wage of labor, w_a, and the MRP_b is equal to the rent

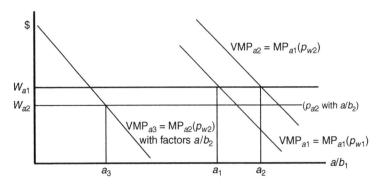

Figure 4.1   The labor market under the opening of trade

of land, Rb. In figure 4.1 we begin with a pre-trade equilibrium featuring the wage, w_{a1}, and the initial demand for
labor, VMP_{a1}. The first, short-term effect of the opening of
trade is an increase in the price of wheat, which shifts the
VMP curve to the right to VMP$a2$.

Because the wheat industry draws its labor from the general, competitive labor market, the price (wage) of factor a
does not rise, but the use of labor increases from a_1 to a_2.
As specified by the Stolper-Samuelson theorem, we must
eventually see the wage decline after trade opens. A little more wheat is demanded for the expanding agricultural
industry, but as the textile industry (which has a comparative
disadvantage) declines, it will release more labor than wheat
will be able to absorb. Figure 4.1 is drawn with various possibilities for factor a combined with a constant amount of
land, giving us a/b_1. In the long run, the new demand for
labor, VMP_3, is to be employed on a new scale of farm. More
land is now used for wheat production (so that we have
a/b_2), and that land is combined with the smaller amount
of labor, b_3, which will be associated with the lower wage
p_{a2} or w_2.

Figure 4.2 shows what happens to the factor land with
the opening of trade, as the price of wheat increases and the
country specializes to increase the output of wheat.

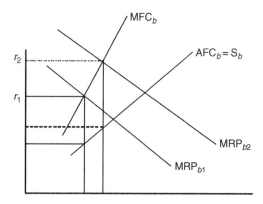

Figure 4.2 Land under the opening of trade

The increasing price of wheat causes landowners to increase the use of land to get larger outputs and this calls for somewhat larger labor inputs, although not as much as will become redundant in the declining textile industry. The demand for land will increase from MRP_{b1} to MRP_{b2} due to the higher price, p_2, and the rental value of the land will rise from r_1 to r_2.

The bilateral monopoly model of factor pricing involves monopsony profits. In labor markets, that profit can be extracted by unions negotiating for a wage equal to the marginal factor cost rather than equal to the wage that would be read off the supply or average factor cost curve under competitive conditions. In the present instance, landholders would grant themselves the higher return to land without the necessity of such negotiations, since they can automatically enjoy the monopsony profits accruing to suppliers in such markets. Before trade, the landowners enjoyed the monopsony profit indicated by the smaller rectangle with solid top and bottom resting on the AFCb line and extending up to r_1. After the marginal revenues derived from wheat sales have increased due to the opening of trade, the monopsony profits will increase to the larger rectangle resting on AFCb and extending up to r_2. This time the rectangle's bottom and top are indicated with dashed lines.

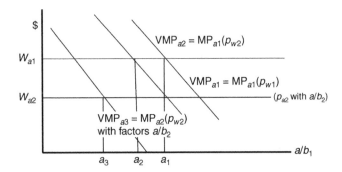

Figure 4.3 Labor in a free trade equilibrium

We can consider the textile industry quickly as well from figure 4.3, which shows the same initial equilibrium for labor as we saw with wages at w_{a1} and output at a_1. The price declines with the opening of trade and the arrival of competitive imports and the country's move toward specialization in wheat as the textile output declines and the use of labor falls to a_2. But in the long run, a will be combined with a smaller, constant amount of land less than b_1, so MP_{a2} will be less than MPa_1. When wages fall generally throughout the economy with the reduced use of labor, w_{a2} will be the new wage for labor and the utilization will be at a_3.

The final case is the reverse of that shown in figure 4.2. Because the demand for land will fall in the textile industry after the country specializes in wheat production, the MRP_b will shift back to the left causing a reduction in land rents, lesser utilization of land as an input in textile production, and smaller monopsonistic profits for landowners. But this will all be more than offset for the landowners with the arrival of specialization in wheat production. These results correspond with those produced by the analysis of Henry George. They tend to reinforce his concern for the well-being of labor and the growing power of monopolized land.

Practical Problems of Protection

George shared a perspective with his readers on the design of tariff policy that was far from a description of prudent consideration by a wise legislature of the needs and circumstances of each industry. Instead, he described the making of a tariff as "simply a great 'grab' in which the retained advocates of selfish interests bully and beg, bribe and logroll, in the endeavor to get the largest possible protection for themselves without regard for other interests or for the general good."[46]

Even in these early times, George described the aim of protection as moving away from the encouragement of infant industries to that of the "home industry," meaning all of the home industries. This was to be seen largely as a product of the political process described earlier. Once protection is initiated, duties will be imposed relentlessly until every industry of sufficient political strength is covered. Once it has begun, the determination to provide "encouragement" for home industry results in a "scramble"[47] that will guarantee the success not of the weak, but of the strong, not of the deserving, but of the unscrupulous. Genuine, infant industries "have no more chance in the struggle for governmental encouragement than infant pigs have with full-grown swine about a meal-tub."[48]

Most perverse about protection are not the trivial inefficiencies, injustice, and misdirection of the policy's design and implementation. It is rather that the policy itself is so misguided and damaging. The protection proffered guarantees a market price that permits inefficiency and noncompetitiveness to produce ingrained apathy and lethargy. Even promising industries that could become competitive in a global economy will ultimately be stunted in their competitive growth.

When students are warned today that protected infant industries generally fail to mature, they need to be instructed that Congress in our time will sometimes put an expiration date on tariffs. That was not apparently the case in the time of George, who described tariff history in the early days of the American Republic, at which time it was asserted that the infant industries, if protected for a few years, would be able to shift for themselves. According to George:

> The infant boys and girls of that time have grown to maturity, become old men and women, and with rare exceptions have passed away. The nation then fringing the Atlantic seaboard has extended across the continent, and instead of four million now numbers nearly sixty million people. But the "infant industries," for which a little temporary protection was then timidly asked, are still infants in their desire for encouragement.[49]

George was successful in his effort not to let the reader forget that this "protection" was really a conspiracy of taxation against the citizens of the country. He was, consequently, offended by protectionist rhetoric, including the demand to reserve the home market for home producers. Reserving that market meant excluding the country's participation in the advantages that beneficial natural conditions or peculiar skills of the people of other countries could provide at relatively low prices. Said he, "If bananas will not grow at home we must not eat bananas. If india-rubber is not a home production we must not avail ourselves of its thousand uses."[50]

Those who will benefit most by and are indoctrinated in favor of protection, of course, convince themselves that tariffs are of general benefit. Their direct financial interest encourages them to be active in spreading their views. Some have ample resources at their disposal, so it is for them a business matter to allocate sufficient funds to propagate their message through whatever public media they can influence. By contrast, those in favor of free trade have no special appeal to any particular interest. And unfortunately, social costs and benefits shared commonly with the general public are far less significant when comparing the personal impact of individual tariff issues. The casual reader of the news fails to appreciate that the implication of such news stories is that Congress and the interests are conspiring to diminish his choices and squeeze his wallet.[51]

Henry George on U.S. Tariff History

Although he made himself conversant with classical trade theory, George as a man of affairs was also keenly interested in the history and politics of international trade. He observed that from the early colonial days, without any protection in place and under British regulations designed to prevent the development of any competitive manufactures, a number of American industries nevertheless took root. In 1789 with the first Tariff Act, the important manufactures of the time, including iron and textiles, were already firmly established. The view that American industry grew with the assistance of protected markets under the wisdom of Hamilton is not one shared by Henry George. The early establishment was without any tariff, and these industries would have continued to grow along with the population whether or not a tariff had ever been established.[52] Moreover, the tariff was a distinct and heavy disadvantage, since it was established across the board and made import prices, the prices of vital production inputs, high enough to destroy any competitive advantages the colonies might have had. These offset, in George's view, the "natural advantages and the inventiveness of our people," since our sales were "confined to our protected market and we can nowhere compete with the manufactures of other countries."

As a result of this inept protection, designed to "keep out foreign importations," the colonies were constrained to import manufactured goods, "while all but a trivial percentage of our exports consist of raw materials."[53] With a mid-nineteenth-century population of nearly 60 million in the United States and with greater consumption of manufactured goods than in any other nation, our export structure left a lot to be desired.

The incomparable advantages of the United States in manufacturing in that era included widely available and accessible coal deposits (surpassing those of any other country) and reservoirs of natural gas supplying fuel with facility and abundance. George considered his country as "the first of civilized nations in the invention and use of machinery, and in the economy of material and labor." Unfortunately, those advantages were "neutralized by the wall of protection we have built along our coasts."[54] While England abandoned protection, the United States redoubled it.

The advent of the Civil War gave a fillip to the forces of protection, and with Americans willing to make any required sacrifice to preserve their union, they were taken advantage of by those anxious to burden them with protective taxes. The ravages of Confederate cruisers along the American coast resulted in high rates of insurance on American ships. Fortunately, the setback on American naval commerce was only temporary, but the bad news was that our protective policy prevented the country from completing the war effort. Rather than regaining a strong position in the world's carrying trade at the end of the war and moving ahead with greater vigor than previously, the United States pursued trade policies that destroyed its competitiveness by preventing Americans from building, and forbidding them to buy, ships. The result was that postbellum commerce declined continuously until American ships became rare phenomena on blue water. George indicated that as a nation of 25 million the United States "plowed every sea of the globe," but as a nation of nearly 60 million after the Civil War, its participation in the carrying trade had effectively been eliminated.[55]

It pained George to see the United States import iron, for example, from Great Britain. Deposits of iron and coal were larger and more easily worked in the United States than in Britain and the United States had actually exported iron to that country before the war. It was the policy of protection that was our undoing. The British abandoned the "repressive system" of protection while the United States availed itself of it more fully, which advantaged the British producer in international commerce vis-à-vis the American producer, whose sales were restricted to the home market. George summarized his point as follows:

> The ores of Spain and Africa which, for some purposes, it is necessary to mix with our own ores, have been burdened with a heavy duty; a heavy duty has enabled a great steel combination to keep steel at a monopoly price; a heavy duty on copper has enabled another combination to get a high price for American copper at home, while exporting it to Great Britain for a low price; and to encourage a single bunting factory the very ensign of an American ship has been subjected to a duty of 150 per cent. From keelson to truck, from the wire in her stays to the brass in her taffrail log, everything that goes to the building, the fitting or the storing of a ship is burdened with heavy taxes. Even should she be repaired abroad she must pay taxes for it on her return home. Thus has protection strangled an industry in which with free trade we might still have led the world. And the injury we have done ourselves has been, in some degree at least, an injury to mankind. Who can doubt that ocean steamers would to-day have been swifter and better had American builders been free to compete with English builders?[56]

The Role of International Trade in George's Message

George believed that his book, *Protection or Free Trade,* had successfully and conclusively demonstrated that only the application of free trade principles could achieve the greatest output and the fairest distribution of wealth. He recognized, of course, that political economists had already demonstrated this repeatedly, so that only special interests and ignorance could ignore the free trade message. But it occurred to him that there was something missing in the whole line of argumentation, since in spite of its powerful appeal to reason, protective sentiment remained very strong and support for it widespread. Proponents of free trade should ask themselves whether the ongoing support for protection was due to the fact that important truths were not generally considered, or because particular errors had not yet been exposed. Perhaps that support should be ascribed to some general incapacity to recognize truth. What do free trade principles prove? Increased productivity and potential gains from specialization and trade do not necessarily demonstrate that the elimination of protection would benefit the working class. George wrote: "The tendency of anything that increases the productive power of labor is to augment wages. But it will not augment wages under conditions in which laborers are forced by competition to offer their services for a mere living."[57] From George's perspective, this argument seemed to invalidate free trade principles. And the frequent resurgence of protectionist sentiment suggested to George that something must strongly commend protection to the popular mind. That is why the protectionist, thoroughly beaten by the logic of the free trade arguments, will almost inevitably come back with an observation demonstrating that the real basis of his belief has remained unscathed. He avers that although free trade may be valid in theory, it fails in practice. Although such a nonsensical answer begs the question, the objection is based on the conviction that free trade arguments simply fail to take account of all the facts.

George felt sympathy for the argument that one might well increase the production of wealth without raising wages or improving the condition of the working classes.[58] George was writing, of course, before a large empirical literature was addressed to this question. One would have to demonstrate convincingly the connection between productive wealth and rising wages, he opined, to gain the support of the working class for free trade. George insisted that workers knew by experience that an increase in wealth in the nation did not mean their living conditions would improve. In the United States the general wealth had increased enormously, but the result was larger fortunes for the rich while labor found it not one whit easier to gain a living. George would not live to experience the effects of economic growth accompanied not only by a decline in protectionism, but also by labor and anti-trust legislation, in a few golden decades of globalization following his death. The progress of his own era he viewed with some skepticism.[59] Because the working class continually had to confront unemployment, sometimes high rates of it, being employed came to be considered a privilege. Protectionism, although it may reduce the power of a community to obtain wealth and enjoy economic growth, offered the ostensible advantage of making work. For the worker, protection must hold out the same promise as the destruction of machinery to those with the Luddite view of the technological displacement of workers. Of this, George wrote:

> Now, should we subject this question to such an examination as we have given to the tariff question we should reach similar results. We should find the notion that invention ought to be restrained as incongruous as the notion that trade ought to be restrained—as incapable of being carried to its logical conclusions without resulting in absurdity.[60]

George's exposition seems to carry an echo of truth to contemporary observation. Even today, the flawless logic promising huge potential benefits of specialization and trade either fails to reach the general public, including organized labor, or fails to convince it that free trade can do anything but harm it. Yet, since George's time, the trickle-down effects of growing productivity, wealth, and incomes associated with the freer trade of the second era of globalization have reached a larger and larger share of the groups that refuse steadfastly to acknowledge that trickle-down can really occur. George himself was perhaps too pessimistic. He was not a systemic pessimist like Marx, since he had great faith that the system of natural liberty could be reformed and would realize its promise through the implementation of his policy prescriptions. He had too little faith perhaps that, even in the absence of his land and tax proposals, the combination of markets and free trade alone could cause economic fortunes to look brighter.

CHAPTER 5

Henry George on Land and Land Policy

Introduction

In California, George had the opportunity to observe first-hand over a period of several years the role of land in the economic development of the state, especially in the area around San Francisco. His observations led him to theorize and write about the role of land in the economic development of the nation. His first attempt in this regard resulted in the publishing of his early work *Our Land and Land Policy* in 1871.

The misery and poverty in the Eastern parts of the United States, which had deeply saddened George, were becoming a part of the development of the younger city of San Francisco. George took it almost as a mission or a calling to find the causes of this unfortunate departure from some natural order of societal progress. He thought about the problem for some time before he found, as he believed, rather sudden, almost revelatory, clarity on the issue. As we saw earlier, that occurred while he was riding a horse in the foothills of Oakland. Although the creative, scholarly rationalization of his beliefs came significantly later, it was that experience that removed all doubt from his mind. It was the phenomenon of land monopolization, the "locking up of the storehouse of nature," that kept the landless, laboring classes from rightful participation in society's progress.

Henry George Jr. recorded that after this experience George "asked no one if he was right: he *knew* he was right" (George, 1900, p. 220). On March 26, 1871, at the age of 32, George sat down to formulate his theory of the issue of land and land policy as it had developed to that point. The effort resulted in a pamphlet that later became a small book.

To this point in his intellectual development, George had never heard of the Physiocrats, the *économistes* in France who were contemporaries of Adam Smith, nor was he aware that they had advocated the imposition of an *impot unique,* a single tax, which they recommended for solving the land problem. George would later insist that he had come closer to the views of Quesnay and his followers than Adam Smith had, although the latter had been personally acquainted with them. George always remembered with some delight the individual who initially informed him of the *économistes* and their policy proposal. This individual was "photographed" on his memory, George wrote, "for, when you have seen a truth that those around you do not see, it is one of the deepest of pleasures to hear of others who have seen it" (ibid., p. 229).

In this area George had the greatest interest, wrote most persuasively and profusely, and exerted the greatest influence on American culture and life. In examining his influence in the area of land policy, we will hopefully also illuminate how and why that influence resulted in a cultural "Georgism" and produced ardent followers properly designated "Georgists."

At the dawn of the twentieth century, the problem of monopoly was among America's major economic preoccupations. That period's brazenly reckless monopolists were commonly referred to as "robber barons"; America was incensed at their callous and exploitative price gouging and abusive practices. A series of acts were legislated early in the 1900s as a response. Earlier, George had been a leading intellect in the attack on the monopolies and the monopolists; he also attacked Congress very articulately for distributing massive tracts of land to the railroad monopolies, thus guaranteeing, in his view, the impoverishment of American workers. The theory is explicated fully in *Our Land and Land Policy* and will be reviewed.

Social Effects of Monopoly in Land

George's theories must be understood as attempting to explain how a growing population and economic growth do not assure progress in the age-old battle against poverty. In George's day the population was growing by about a million per year and the large surplus of American land was being distributed very rapidly. Huge land grants were made to the railroads, leading to increasing ownership for a select few, while there was much less land available for the benefit of the general populace. Moreover, the increasing value of land was not productive of widespread prosperity.

The policy supposition was that the government's land grants to the railroads would hasten the building of the railroads. George, however, contended that in California those grants had actually retarded railroad construction, since they retarded the actual settlement of the lands granted. George was convinced that the grants were made to individuals who generally had neither the means nor the intention to build. Lands were simply held as long as necessary before being sold to others who would ultimately find it profitable to build (George, 1902, p. 29).

But George found that giving a land grant for the building of a railroad and getting it built before private enterprise would have done it without the intervention was not the normal experience. And even if a railroad was built, the land was given for nothing; capital was simply diverted from more market responsive to less productive public investments, and society was the poorer for it. Whether or not a railroad was built, the land grant tended to disperse population and to promote land monopolization. Both of those effects made many poorer, and a few much richer, so giving away from 12 to 25,000 acres of land for each mile of road to be constructed was for George an inexcusable, "wicked extravagance."[1]

It was not as though a single speculator were monopolizing the land, but the aggregate effect of speculators was the removal of land from immediate use. If speculation were not practiced, individuals would be acquiring land they intended to use; unused land would have no value, at least not at prices above that which the state charged. As land use increased with societal progress, it would gain value if it possessed more natural advantages than unoccupied land, or if it were in a central location. These characteristics endow land with real value, while monopolization confers what George referred to as unnecessary or fictitious value.[2]

For George, sharing in mankind's ownership of land was as essential a right of the individual as personal freedom. Without access to land, no man could be assured of the right to life, liberty, and the pursuit of happiness. Thus, he concludes that each of God's children has an inherent right to share in all the natural abundance of the earth or under or above the earth (he subsumed all natural physical resources under the title "land").

What a man produces is his property—it is rightfully his own, to use, sell, or bequeath as he sees fit. Man's very existence also entitles him to the use of as much of nature's free gifts as is necessary to meet his wants and needs, so long as he does not interfere with the equal rights of his fellows.[3] This natural right cannot be alienated from him; it is God's free gift to every individual who is born. To George, this right was as sacred, as indefeasible as the right to life itself. But it is important also to note that as every man has a natural right to that land which he requires for his own needs, no man has a right to any more than that amount. To deny this is to acknowledge the "atrocious doctrine" that the Creator intended some men to be masters and some to be slaves.[4] Permitting one man to monopolize the land that would have been available for the support of others is to permit the monopolist to appropriate the labor of those others; it is effectually an appropriation of their very lives and is tantamount to instituting slavery.

George returned several times in his writing to the notion that taking a man's right of access to the land that God had given to all men was, in essence, to make him a slave. For without land he became dependent upon his labor to satisfy his wants and needs, and the owner of land could use his resource to command the labor he desired to enrich himself. But slavery was actually somewhat better than when monopolized land permitted the exploitation of the worker. Competition drives wages down to a minimum where monopolized land and deadly competitive labor markets enslave workers.

Under traditional slavery the slave owner is bound by social mores and traditions to provide the slave with better living conditions, personal security, and the human dignity that is the concomitant of such things. Slavery left people better off than George found them, for example, in the ghettos of the laborers in England. George concluded that the land problem was at the core of the social problems of poverty and unequal distribution of wealth. Again, inept land policy increases the incidence of poverty even in the midst of dynamic processes of economic growth and development.

George did not hesitate to take the founding fathers to task for having helped the country march down this path of progress and poverty. Although he admired them for having raised the American temple of civil and religious liberty, he faulted them for their treatment of land, which he correctly viewed as the foundation of the country's economic institutions at that time. The importance of land and land policy they seem never to have perceived. "In a new country where nothing was so abundant as land, and where there was nothing to suggest its monopolization, the men who gave direction to our thought and shaped our polity shook off the idea of the divine right of kings without shaking off that of the divine right of landowners," he wrote. So in framing the great truth that all men are born with equal rights to life, liberty, and the pursuit of happiness, they missed the implications of leaving access to the land out of the equation. Access to the land would, in practice, give laborers the means to life, liberty, and happiness "as a living reality." Thus, they instituted a form of government founded on the principles of independence and virtue for the people, but did not eliminate the possibility of land monopolization. With that opportunity open to the opportunistic and the privileged, there was no institutional structure in place that could "keep the masses virtuous and independent." The fathers thus "laid the foundations for a glorious house; but they laid them in the sand."[5]

When George reached the end of this treatise on land and land policy, he formulated his conclusions about the broader implications of American land policy of that time. Those conclusions make the title he chose for the book seem inadequate, since it reaches beyond land policy to issues of railroads, speculation, land grants, and land monopolization. Considering the impact of those issues on government policies more generally, including taxation, it is apparent that he was really addressing the impacts of U.S. land policy on society and civilization. Perhaps he should have titled the book *Land, Land Policy, and American Civilization,* making the title of the book indicate the work's true scope.

As we have already seen in an earlier chapter, George is viewed by those who have little acquaintance with his work as a radical figure fighting against private property in land. It is true, as this work graphically shows us, that he was opposed to it. But he recognized that an attempt to roll back the rights that had already been distributed in our society would be more than disruptive. One of the reasons he so strongly favored the single tax was that it would end land monopolization and speculation, accomplishing the same ends as an elimination of private land ownership.

Again, George was supportive of markets and of free enterprise. As most individuals who realistically support them, George was realistic. He perceived clearly that markets require regulation and that capitalists need institutional restraints to spare customers, workers, and fellow citizens from the dishonest and fraudulent among the numbers of market actors. He likewise recognized that markets do not drive the public sector and that supplying public services requires public finance (although hardly the financial manipulation of public sector unions that monopolize to exploit their fellow countrymen today). The single tax would be necessary not only to eliminate the ongoing concentration of land ownership, but to supply the revenues to perform the functions of the state formerly financed by all the other taxes George wanted to eliminate.

Those who might expect George to support more statist economic action should note that he was not advocating more government; it was his view that his age had seen too much government. "It is a truth that cannot be too clearly kept in mind that the best government is that which governs least, and that the more a republican government undertakes to do, the less republican it becomes. Unhealthy social conditions are but the result of interferences with natural rights."[6]

On the fourth of July 1877, in the California Theatre in San Francisco, George gave an oration entitled "The American Republic: Its Dangers and Possibilities" that demonstrated how American land policy and politics generated the poverty that George feared was growing in the country.[7] He pleaded that the poverty suffered by most was not the product of their own individual faults, but of conditions society imposes upon them. He felt, however, that poverty was in fact a crime—not an individual but a social crime, "for which all the participants in our democracy are responsible."[8]

George was convinced, as we have seen, that concentrated land ownership permitted land owners to appropriate some share of the earnings of others. This "robbery of labor" degrades the laborer and disadvantages him in labor markets. It diminishes production and produces unnecessary poverty. This growing "disparity of social conditions" arises from laws that thwart the equal rights of men.[9]

George expressed his belief that in a genuinely Christian community, "in a society that honoured not with the lips but with the act, the doctrines of Jesus, no one would have occasion to worry about physical needs any more than do the lilies of the field. There is enough and to spare."[10] This poverty springs from a primary injustice that made life more difficult for workers in George's day than it had been, for example, five centuries earlier. The history of England clearly shows the reason. For several centuries, a parliament composed of aristocrats and employers passed laws vainly endeavoring to reduce wages. But workers could not be reduced to a subsistence living simply because they retained access to the bounty of nature, namely, to the land. The country still recognized the truth that all men had equal rights to the earth. The land held in private possession was held only on a tenure granted by the nation, and for rent owed to the nation.

England had no national debt at that time. Centuries of wars were conducted at the charge of the landowners. And everywhere there were lands held in common for everyone in the community. Once those lands were enclosed, the commons gradually monopolized, the church lands transferred into the grasp of greedy nobles, and the crown lands turned over as the private and absolute property of the king's favorites; thus, poverty began to deepen in England. In the same manner it was gaining sway in the United States of that time.[11] Where workers have access to land, if they cannot find an employer, they can employ themselves. When they are denied such access, they must compete with each other for the wages of an employer. Thus, the laborers had been robbed of the natural opportunity of employing themselves; they could not find a piece of land on which to work without paying someone else for the privilege. You may institute all the reforms you desire, George protested, but the only result would be that the land would increase in value. The price that some must pay others for the privilege of living would simply rise.[12]

George asked: Where could a man get a title making the earth his personal property? In his view, the right to property was sacred because it was ordained by the laws of nature, or by the laws of God if you will, and because it was necessary to social order and civilization. Man has a right to property concerning the things produced by his own labor. The right against all the world, "to give or to keep, to lend, to sell or to bequeath; but how can he get such a right to land when it was here before he came? Individual claims to land rest only on appropriation."[13]

A religion that does not assert the natural rights of man cannot be Christianity. The latter, George vehemently insisted, has no protest when the earth, "created by the Almighty as a dwelling-place for all his children," becomes the exclusive property of a small, opportunistic subset of them. When this common historical phenomenon is observed, all of God's other children are denied their birthright. To George, this was a travesty. A Christian in a democratic society must see to it as a citizen and a lawmaker that we become a genuinely Christian society. To do so, we must return to the Declaration of Independence, which guarantees the equal right to life, liberty, and the pursuit of happiness. But does it not also involve the "equal right to land, without which neither life, liberty, nor the freedom to pursue happiness is possible?"[14]

Although George found the situation of the working poor intolerable and felt that it was becoming more desperate with the passage of time and the growing concentration of land ownership and industry, he was not a pessimist. He was convinced that he had the solution to the problem of poverty and believed that society's obvious progress could be distributed more happily through his simple policy prescription, namely, the implementation of the single tax. An acquaintance with his writings would almost permit one to describe George as a Christian utopian, were his occasional references to Christianity and his bent for dramatic oratory not so thoroughly subordinated to his scholarly reasoning.

George wrote in a highly rhetorical style in his later work *Social Problems*—even more so than was occasionally evident in *Progress and Poverty*. In that later work, he insisted that a civilization capable of concentrating power and wealth in the hands of a select minority, rendering the remainder no better than "human machines," must ultimately produce anarchy and destruction. At the same time, a civilization could actually produce, even for the poorest, all the comforts and conveniences currently available only for the rich.[15] He envisioned this society in which prisons and almshouses would disappear and charities would become unnecessary. Such a society was simply waiting for "social intelligence that will adapt means to ends."[16] He and his followers, of course, had already discovered and illuminated the path.

That George seemed to perceive this as almost a Christian utopia can be inferred from the same source. He wrote, namely, that society's hope for "the free, full development of humanity, is in the gospel of brotherhood—the gospel of Christ."[17] He expressed the sentiment that one observing the law and taking proper care of his family, but who is not concerned about the welfare of his fellow citizens and particularly of the poor, whether or not he may sometimes "bestow alms," can be considered neither a "true Christian" nor a good citizen.

Economic Conditions Suggesting, to George, the Single Tax

Surging Economic Development. George was convinced that the discovery and invention of one period stimulate that of the next. George believed that the industrial progress of the previous half century was destined to pale before that of the next and Americans could scarcely conceive of the future George saw opening before them. The people of his age were witnessing the passing of the world's center of learning, art, and wealth to the western side of the Atlantic. The most significant parts of this blossoming of economic development were the surging processes of industrialization, the increasingly complex division of labor, and the concentration of wealth and power in large firms. George (1883, p. 17) marveled at

> how readily the railroad companies, the coal operators, the steel producers, even the match manufacturers, combine, either to regulate prices or to use the powers of government. The tendency in all branches of industry is to the formation of rings against which the individual is helpless, and which exert their power upon government whenever their interests may thus be served.

Government, Industry, and Wall Street. With insight that seems to adumbrate even the proclivities of the powerful players of our own day, George described the financial interaction of industry and Wall Street to the role of the government, the great provider of subsidies and of the tax and regulatory environments:

> Great aggregations of wealth, whether individual or corporate, tend to corrupt government and take it out of

the control of the masses of the people . . . . . . Great wealth always supports the party in power, no matter how corrupt it may be. It never exerts itself for reform, for it instinctively fears change. It never struggles against misgovernment. When threatened by the holders of political power it does not agitate, nor appeal to the people; it buys them off. It is in this way, no less than by its direct interference, that aggregated wealth corrupts government, and helps to make politics a trade. Our organized lobbies, both legislative and Congressional, rely as much upon the fears as upon the hopes of moneyed interests.[18]

Immigration and Population Growth. The population's natural growth was bolstered by the massive emigration from Europe, which George (1883, p. 24) described as "the greatest migration of peoples since the world began." The internal migration from east to west was even greater; the westward flow experienced at Chicago, St. Paul, Kansas City, and Omaha had at that time increased rather than diminished. Nevertheless, natural population growth was experiencing even greater expansion.

The Unavailability of Land for New Settlers. George wrote of emigrants passing over long stretches of vacant lands from Manhattan Island to the Far West without finding a spot available for settlement. There was abundant land available in Manhattan, for example, but its people were "packed closer than anywhere else in the world." Its abundance was due to the fact that Manhattan real estate had already been appropriated. Much of the population that could not be accommodated by the land came from Europe where the continent's poor were forced out because the land in Europe, scarcely all in use, had all been appropriated by the landholding classes. Absentee European landowners had likewise appropriated a large share of America's land. It has already been noted that Congress had been anxious to distribute gargantuan parcels of land to the railroads, which were then often passed on to agents and agencies that would concentrate land ownership, placing it out of the reach of most immigrants. George (1883, p. 27) foresaw that the remaining American lands would for a long period of time not come into use, but would quite soon all be "fenced in." The swelling population would soon occupy those remaining lands, effecting an increase in the price of even the poorest land worth settling to a point hitherto unknown.

After discussing the disappearance of what should not only be available, but also essentially free land for social expansion and development, George wrote of the development of the factory/industrial system, which took away the independence of the worker and made him dependent on a social order he could neither understand nor control. Ideas, for example, of social alienation, which occurred mostly to Marx and other Europeans, are also discussed by George under the rubric of the problems of landless labor. He then turns to the problem of urbanization.

The Effects on People of Urbanization and Industrialization. When the first U.S. census was taken in 1790, the country's cities contained no more than 3.3 percent of the total population. By 1880, cities contained 22.5 percent of the population, demonstrating a tendency of the populace to concentrate. Like industrial and agricultural concentration, this urbanization was one of the chief characteristics of the age. All over the civilized world the growth of the larger cities was outstripping population growth (George, 1883, p. 40).

During the onset of the feudal age, free proprietors had been converted into vassals. All of society had been subordinated to a hierarchy of privilege and wealth. George saw a similar change occurring in his own time. A new aristocracy based on land ownership was developing; whether ownership was based on heredity or chance made little difference in America, George observed,[19] since there were few prizes to be distributed in this lottery. As in any lottery, the vast majority of its participants were destined to draw blanks. America's poor adjusted to this reality quite readily, since they and the more fortunate few were indoctrinated with the view that it is natural that some will be poor and some rich, and that the growing inequalities in the distribution of wealth did in no way impugn our institutions. That perspective, wrote George, "pervades our literature, and is taught in the press, in the church, in school and in college."[20]

According to George, when generous earnings begin to roll up into growing fortunes, the most superficial investigation will always discover some element of monopoly present, "some appropriation of wealth produced by others." Usually, there will be no trace of superior effort, sacrifice, or skill behind the growing affluence, but generally just better luck or greater unscrupulousness. The "element of monopoly, of appropriation and spoliation will, when we come to analyze them, be found largely to account for all great fortunes."[21]

George provides examples of rich individuals whose fortunes were not derived from hard work and sacrifice, although some of them began their path to fortune with those virtues. One of those he wrote about was Jay Gould, whose fortune building got its first start by superior industry and self-denial. But the really big money came later from "wrecking railroads, buying judges, corrupting legislatures, getting up rings and pools and combinations to raise or depress stock values and transportation rates."[22] Whenever fortunes are built through increasing land values, George insisted, it is because someone successfully appropriates the power to take a larger share of wealth produced by the labor of others. George asks rhetorically what we should call someone who tells us that God would have us be content with such a world.

He simply saw no need for the kind of poverty experienced in Western society, which clearly has inexhaustible capabilities and resources; if society were guided by honest intelligence, all material wants could be satisfied. But if we refuse to apply the intelligence that can adapt social organization to "natural laws," allowing monopolies to capture more resources than they can use, or permit power and cunning to rob "honest labor," all the social evils and chronic poverty cannot be avoided by any policy means. According to George, permitting such conditions to persist might well guarantee poverty in paradise.[23]

George eloquently expressed his conviction that only injustice prevents us from overcoming poverty. In his words (George, 1883, p. 74):

> Consider the enormous powers of production now going to waste; consider the great number of unproductive consumers maintained at the expense of producers—the rich men and dudes, the worse than useless government officials, the pickpockets, burglars and confidence men; the highly respectable thieves who carry on their operations inside the law; the great army of lawyers; the beggars and paupers, and inmates of prisons; the monopolists and cornerers and gamblers of every kind and grade. Consider how much brains and energy and capital are devoted, not to the production of wealth, but to the grabbing of wealth. Consider the waste caused by competition which does not increase wealth; by laws which restrict production and exchange. Consider how human power is lessened by insufficient food, by unwholesome lodgings, by work done under conditions that produce disease and shorten life. Consider how intemperance and unthrift follow poverty. Consider how the ignorance bred of poverty lessens production, and how the vice bred of poverty causes destruction, and who can doubt that under conditions of social justice all might be rich?[24]

A few pages later, George demonstrated with his proposed policy and economic order prescriptions that he was not the socialist that some have taken him for. He contended, namely, that a policy of forcible wealth redistribution, with a massive transfer to the "have nots," would do "great injustice: we would work great harm."[25] Moreover, from the instant such a policy were undertaken, tendencies observed in the previous unjust inequalities would start to reassert themselves. Before long, they would be as gross as they had previously been. The cure for the social disease of poverty, George argued, was to remove the *causes* of the inequitable distribution of wealth.

Redistribution is a terrible disincentive to the production of wealth, one that George tried always to discourage. Whatever any rich man really produced, no matter how large the increment to justly accrued assets, George would have him retain, placing no limits on what an individual might acquire. It would be enough to improve the lot of the unfortunate numbers of mankind to remove the possibility of fraud, monopolization, and inept policy from impoverishing their victims.

Ireland represents for George an example of the abuses that created and perpetuated the poverty and degradation that typified that country. But George held that the system that doomed the pauperized Irish masses had greater sway in the United States of his day than it did in Ireland (George, 1883, p. 104). He railed against the rape of Ireland by England, establishing and maintaining English landlords to control the destinies of the Irish *Untermenschen* (not a Georgist term) by owning the land and confiscating its surplus for themselves. George saw those same landlords sending their criminals and impoverished to our shores, but also buying land on a massive scale in America, thus putting themselves in a position to harvest even larger rents from their holdings in the United States, while dooming America's non-landed class to poverty and misery.

In today's post-agricultural society, land is no longer the key element for wealth George perceived it to be in his time. The key today for an initial access to wealth is education and the learned skills that enhance productivity for an industrial/postindustrial, services/information society. Education can do for the individual what holding some amount of land could have done in the past. Nevertheless, land still has great value; if the unemployed of our day still had or could gain access to land, such as was historically the case in England before the closing of the commons, they would have the means to sustain themselves even in the face of high general unemployment. Today, we choose instead to take care of the poor through state subsidies and transfer payments.

At least in part, the poor remain so today, as George observed, because the government permits their abuse through the distribution of monopoly privileges on the basis of political patronage and cronyism to those whom governmental agents select for wealth and privilege. As an example of the state's establishment or promotion of monopolies, George favored the case of the railroads in the United States and Great Britain, as well as in some other countries. In the United States, he complained,

> where railroads are of more importance than in any other country in the world, our only recognition of their public character has been in the donation of lands and the granting of subsidies, which have been the cause of much corruption, and in some feeble attempts to regulate fares and freights.[26]

In George's day the direct taxes of local governments, that is, the states, counties, and municipalities, exceeded the aggregate taxation of the Federal government, and local taxes were generally levied on real and personal property. Taxes falling on improvements to land operated as a deterrent to production, George held. Land that had been developed was consistently assessed at higher values than unused land of the same quality.[27] Once again, taxes levied on land improvements will tend to discourage the use of such land for production, representing the disincentive that George was anxious to combat. Taxes reducing the bottom line on investment returns encourage a search for better returns on capital elsewhere.

From Slavery to More Serious Poverty. George argued quite seriously in his book *Social Problems,* as in other places, that the phenomenon of slavery was sometimes less harsh than the poverty experienced by the oppressed laboring classes when land was concentrated under the ownership of the privileged. As observed earlier, if labor always had access to lands that could be farmed by the unemployed, the depressing outcomes described in *Progress and Poverty* could be avoided. If such lands were available, industrial conflicts would not find the workers without advantages. Employers would not find anxious unemployed workers desperate for employment. Finding all labor already employed, managers would have to offer higher wages than the workers could already make for themselves (George, 1883, p. 122).

George cited the Massachusetts Bureau of Labor Statistics and the Illinois Bureau of Labor Statistics to show that in a majority of cases the earnings of wage workers failed to sustain the workers' families, so that it was necessary for both women and children to supplement the family head's wages with their earnings. Even in the more affluent states of that day, men were reduced to a "virtual peonage," living in their employer's housing, trading at their employer's stores, and generally incapable of escaping their own indebtedness. In New York, women worked from 14 to 16 hours a day, George observed, averaging no more than $3 or $4 a week. And this was certainly not the lowest-paying city. "As a matter of dollars and cents," he wrote, "no master could afford to work slaves so hard and keep them so cheaply."[28]

Southern slavery, only recently overcome in the United States of Henry George, was described by him as the "coarser form of slavery." This system, in which each slave was the property of a particular owner, was fitted only for a rude state of society, demanding increasingly greater trouble and expense for the owner. The slaves had to be provided with minimally suitable shelter, nutrition, and clothing. By shifting property to land and away from slaves, the proprietary class was saved much expense, including the costs of supervision. Land ownership still makes it possible for the owner, even if no individual slaves are owned, to appropriate the worker's labor as before.

Georgists and Georgism

George's gift for writing, his ability to infect others with his own burning convictions, and his criticism of and approach to specific, difficult economic issues worked together to win him many, many readers, many admirers, and even a significant number of ardent followers. Usually, the ardent followers were more interested in political change than in the academic arguments advanced in advocacy. In any case, *Progress and Poverty* was one of the most popular books in the United States and Europe for decades; it was by far the most widely read book on economics.

Before delving into the question of George and the "Georgists," his ardent followers, it is worthwhile to pause and note that George also had some influence on the academic lights of his profession. This is somewhat surprising, since the academic community of economists, both in the United States and in England, was mostly rather horrified that an untrained individual such as Henry George could receive so much attention, even from nonacademic readers. These economists were also incensed at the deprecation heaped upon them by George's writings, so most of them opposed his work vigorously.

From the perspective of the academy, George's theory was not only wrong, but also outdated. In England, Marshall was building conceptual bridges toward a more modern theory that would move the profession beyond its classical foundations. In America, some of the leading intellects were clearly influenced by George. These academics were not inclined, of course, to be Georgists, since he was merely an amateur whose writings did not reflect work done at the cutting edge of the profession.

In an earlier chapter, it was suggested that George influenced others in the profession. Among these it is important to mention John Bates Clark, credited with being one of the founders of "marginal" analysis. Henry George would likely have approved of this designation, not because of the way calculus addressed incremental values as "marginal," but because of what he believed its value added to economic analysis.

John Bates Clark based his formulation of the marginal productivity theory of income distribution on George's theory of rent. Clark and George did not share the same objectives when attempting to explain the distribution of income. George represented classicism while anticipating the much later development of institutional economics, and he remained disinterested in the marginalist revolution. Nevertheless, George and Clark did have some common interests. Early on, Clark wrote from a socioeconomic perspective based on populist viewpoints similar to those of George, sharing George's sympathy for the goals of labor unions as well as his distaste for socialism.

But all this related to a world that felt George's work did not fit and George remained perfectly happy not to be a part of that world. George wanted his theory to serve as the foundation of action and implemented policies. George's avid followers who share that desire are "Georgists." These individuals are concerned with far more than the relevance and substance of George's economic theory. They share his sense of justice and desire for a tax system that yields Georgist outcomes. It is not unfair to assert, as Heavey (2003) has done, that something of a religious fervor is inherent to Georgism. Those who do not "share the faith," especially academics, would be inclined to see Georgists as zealots. In any case, they would suspect that Georgist enthusiasm may tend to "narrow the field of vision," as Heavey suggests.

Georgists in the United States

One Georgist (DeNigris, 2007) has given a very readable account of what Georgists and sympathetic policymakers around the world have accomplished in the spirit of Henry George. Of Georgist policy endeavors, a relatively successful campaign came in 1896, in Delaware. The "Single Taxers," as Georgists came to be called, focused their attention on Delaware due to its diminutive size and proximity to Philadelphia and New York, where the movement was strongest. The campaign's intent, under Louis Freeland Post, Thomas Shearman, and Lawson Purdy, was to win the governorship and take over the legislature. If the single tax theory could successfully be applied in one state, it could then possibly become a national issue. The results of that election, however, were indicative of the likelihood that Georgism could become a powerful national phenomenon. The Single Taxers lost, receiving only 3 percent of the vote.

Following the 1896 failure of the movement at the state level in Delaware, the movement attempted to establish the single tax at the municipal level. In 1900, the sculptor Frank Stephens, the architect Will Price, and the soap manufacturer Joseph Fels purchased 162 acres of land in north Wilmington, Delaware, to create the Village of Arden (named after the "Forest of Arden" in William Shakespeare's *As You Like It*). The experiment was less geared to implementing a single tax than to establishing common ownership of the community's land, of which more than 50 percent was held in common for general use.

Ardentown, a second village created in 1922, was followed by Ardencroft in 1950. All three villages are based on the single tax, but they also offer more to their residents than just the tax experiment. Georgists point out that this system of land-valued tax can function in an urban setting and that it is used widely.

In the United States, Delaware (with its three Ardens), Pennsylvania, Alabama (with its Fairhope, the first single tax community in the country in 1895), California, and Alaska all apply some type of land-based tax to at least some of the areas within their borders. Alaska taxes oil lands in the vicinity of Prudhoe Bay. California taxes over 100 farmland districts by land value. And in Pennsylvania, DeNigris (2007, p. 23) found that 15 cities apply a "graded tax plan". The Center for the Study of Economics in Philadelphia (see www.urbantools.org) indicates there are now 17 jurisdictions that apply a graded tax plan.

The appendix to this chapter suggests numerous websites that chronicle the work of Georgists in our time and in the past. It provides suggested literature for the reader interested in knowing more about the policy reform efforts of some of the Georgists, in the United States, the United Kingdom, and numerous other countries.

Georgist Influence in the United Kingdom

Douglas (1999) provides a competent and succinct review of the highlights of Georgist influence in England, Ireland, and Scotland. According to him, by the time George's name was evoked in connection with a tax matter in the United Kingdom, it had already become widely known. When George's works, especially *Progress and Poverty* (1879) and *The Irish Land Question* (1881),[29] appeared in England, the Irish Land War was already beginning to leave lasting impacts on British politics.

The Land Reform Association was established in 1883 and reconstituted as the English Land Restoration League in 1884. The Scottish Land Restoration League was also formed in the latter year. Both organizations were soon publishing and promoting George's ideas; lecture tours featuring the American speaker were also organized. During the last two decades of the nineteenth century, George's ideas were taking British radicals by storm and many of the radical workforce had copies of *Progress and Poverty* on their bookshelves.

Many radicals were more Georgist than socialist in the modern sense. George Bernard Shaw and Philip Snowden were among those who contrived to support both Georgist and socialist ideas, regardless of how incompatible they really were. Douglas writes as an example of the conflict involved here, that many came to understand land nationalization to mean the direct control of land use and even land seizures by the state, whether or not any compensation was involved. That socialist position may have been a strong temptation to George, given his views regarding the evil effects of land concentration and of the loss of access to the land by the laboring classes. But George's clear position on the issue was that only the *rent* of the land should be appropriated by the state through a tax on land values. Some of the socialists who credited George with their conversion to the movement, likewise falsely attributed to him in their own minds the willingness to confiscate land from the large landholders.

This was all established history when the Chancellor of the Exchequer David Lloyd George introduced one of the most famous fiscal measures in British history, the "People's Budget" of 1909. The budget was designed to raise more money from taxation for the "naval race" that occupied Britain and Germany at the time and for Britain's first "old-age pensions." The budget included a direct income tax, including a new, progressive surcharge on higher incomes, car and gas levies to pay for road construction, and increased inheritance taxes. But the budget was particularly notable for a 20 percent tax on the capital gain of land when it changed hands and for a small levy on all underdeveloped land and minerals! As a result of George's widely known writings and lectures, together with David Lloyd George's highly visible budget, almost everyone in Britain was well acquainted with Henry George's views in this prewar period. Interestingly, Alfred Marshall was also a public supporter of the George Budget of 1909.

Georgists and their Influence in Europe, South Africa, Australia, and Canada

In Denmark, 50 percent of governmental revenue is generated by land-value taxation. The local governments of both New Zealand and South Africa implement the single tax. All six states and a majority of the municipalities of Australia tax land values, although an exemption of improvements to the land and to structures on it, an essential part of George's doctrine, is not universally applied. In several of the western cities of Canada, land values are taxed at a higher rate than improvements.

Georgist Influence in Germany

Backhaus (1997) tells us that some of Henry George's basic ideas had preceded him and taken root in Germany even before the appearance of George's books in that country. Land reform became the central issue for a German intellectual and political movement. It is interesting that Germany's tax legislation in the Georgist spirit was addressed not to land taxation but to the income tax and its connection with business investment decisions, especially real estate investment.

When *Progress and Poverty* appeared in 1880 it was greeted with widespread approbation, but it was acknowledged for the author's conviction rather than the originality of the single tax notion. The Germans generally contend that William Ogilvie first proposed the single tax, followed by both James and John Stuart Mill. But the famous early German economist Friedrich List (1845) is also credited with clear advocacy of the doctrine.

On the practical side of German affairs, Michael Flürschein, the manager of an Iron Works in Gaggenau, was arguing at the time of Henry George for land reform. He produced several pamphlets and a monthly paper, *Deutsches Land,* which led to the formation in 1888 of the *Deutscher Bund fuer Bodenbesitzreform.*

By 1910, at least 652 municipalities and counties in the German Reich had actually adopted a "land added value tax" (Backhaus, 1997). Frankfurt am Main was the first German city to do so in 1894. The German Reich instituted such a tax in 1911, which replaced specific state taxes in Hamburg, Lübeck, Lippe, Hesse, and other states. This tax was complex and difficult to implement as the municipalities and counties shared in the revenue according to different formulae. Even worse, it added so little to the tax yield for the Reich that after only two years, in 1913, the Reich agreed to restore the relevant taxing authority to the municipalities and counties. Thereafter, the Reich turned to taxation of wealth; the land tax act remained on the books, but was no longer in effect.

Even after the Reich's 1913 abandonment of its own land taxation and its assignment of the revenues to the counties and municipalities, the different states still had quite different systems and municipal autonomy was *not* especially strong in this period. Land taxation, nevertheless, had an important common characteristic across the German lands: it was independent of realized income from the land. Set charges were established for each piece of land that, in a general (admittedly somewhat tenuous) sense, was an approximation of the land rent and taxation of that rent rather than the improvements to the land (Backhaus, 1997, p. 13).

Real estate taxation in Germany is currently subject to competitive legislation, which means that either the federal government or one of the 16 constituent *Bundesländer* (states) can legislate. If both the states and federal government legislate, however, the federal government's laws prevail. Remaining from the era of the German Reich is the practice of assigning the tax revenue to the municipalities and counties, with the prerogative of tax legislation retained by central authority and the tax rates established locally.

The income tax code permits the deduction of commercial losses, including where such "losses" can be shown to have been incurred by making (e.g., real estate) investments, the returns from which appear only over the long term. Moreover, by permitting accelerated depreciations along with these deductions, the yield from the investments becomes tax-free. The wealth created through the investments also remain tax free if those investments (as specified by the income tax code) continue indefinitely.

Permitting high-income earners to invest in specific (especially developmentally critical) areas, German economic recovery received a strong stimulus. Investors escaped income tax by reinvesting their income in preferred investment areas (housing, real estate development, shipping, etc.). Those areas could thus access a supply of credit limited only by the incomes of these high-income earners.

The same techniques were applied when the Federal Republic was reunited and it was necessary to reconstruct East Germany. In its accommodation of reunification, the European Union exempted Germany from EU tax harmonization. Backhaus tells us that these unique "Georgist" elements in the German income tax system make it too divergent to fit the process of "harmonization before the reconstruction of Eastern Germany has been completed."[30] This "Georgist" stipulation that land rent be taxed totally whereas the associated improvements remain untaxed, favors economic efficiency over equity, which Backhaus says is characteristic of real estate taxation in Germany.

What does it mean to be a Georgist?

Robert V. Andelson (2004) contends that being a Georgist "in the larger sense" does not require subscribing to everything Henry George penned as holy writ. Nor must a Georgist believe that no aspect of George's system may be questioned. Andelson accepts as Georgist one who generally believes that with respect to the most vital points, "more than any other single social ethicist or political economist, George had it right." That some of George's ideas are flawed or even simply outdated does not diminish his stature, neither for Andelson nor for this author. Many who are not sufficiently acquainted with George's works assume that he was far less informed and sophisticated than was actually the case.

The legacies of great economists have not been completed truths perfected beyond modification or amelioration. Those who admire the great thinkers of the past recognize that scholars begin their work each generation standing on the shoulders of the generations of great minds who preceded them. And even without having completed the search for truth, the great minds of the past have impacted, for good or ill, the development of public policies.

Georgists susceptible to being characterized as true believers may not recognize all of the policy outcomes reflective of George's influence, since they were not brought to fruition under the banner of his name. In the next chapter we will trace some of the influences of George's thought to areas of economic research as perceived not by Georgists, but by economists who have respected his work and perceived its influence on the development of economic analysis beyond George's time.

Naturally, a Georgist must be less than perfectly comfortable with this perspective. Those whose lives are intertwined with the movement have been led to hope for something far more dramatic than to see intellectual evidence that George is considered by many economists to have been a serious thinker. Mark A. Sullivan, Secretary and Administrative Director of the Robert Schalkenbach Foundation, also former President of the Council of Georgist Organizations, which includes over 30 usually small and informal organizations, would be an example of a Georgist whose personal interest in and affiliation with the movement go back many years. Sullivan was introduced to Georgist ideas early in his life and enjoyed the guidance of some of what he describes as the movement's elder statesmen. After many years of activity on the part of Georgist organizations, Sullivan (2003) has joined others in an academic discussion asking why the movement has not been more successful and what it would take for it to become so. It seems likely that men of affairs find it more difficult than academicians to be patient in the long wait for good ideas to have some significant impact on public life.

But the Georgists are engaged in not only academic discussions. Many are engaged in policy initiatives on tax reform at the state and municipal levels. They continue to teach good economics to local legislators and officers. They are often practical and persuasive men of affairs. In a recent e-mail to me, H. William Batt (2011) summarized the principal lines of argumentation Georgists present routinely to local decision makers in discussion of tax reform (Dr. Batt's words are in quotes):

- "The market value of urban land is sufficient to provide a tax base to support all the public services for a city, a conclusion that has come to be known as the Henry George Theorem." The original argument by George was that a nation could drop all other taxes and meet its financial obligations relying on receipts of land rents through the single tax alone. At the local level an appealing argument can be made that a city could drop all other forms of taxation, including the normal property tax that taxes improvements on the land, by properly taxing nothing more than the rental value of the land itself. "A tax on the economic rents from natural resources has sufficient capacity to supplant all the conventional taxes on goods and labor, and pay for all the public services which governments are asked to provide. It may even be possible to pay a citizens' dividend from such rents were they recovered by the public."

- "Since the market value of economic rents is socially created, it offers the soundest moral basis for taxation."
- "A tax on economic rents offers an opportunity for the community to recover its 'commons' which has over the course of years been erroneously privatized."
- For the next point, we should remember that "land" for George and the Georgists includes not only the land itself, but all the natural resources associated with it, for example, the forests, oil deposits, and other minerals et cetera. These resources are given by nature or nature's creator not alone to those individuals who may confiscate them from the rest of society and then pass them on to their heirs in perpetuity, but to all men equally.

> Natural resource titles should be regarded as usufructuary leaseholds rather than fee simple property. The freehold ownership of land in any form is a form of theft and is the moral equivalent of owning slaves. Use rights are every bit as harmonious with contemporary society as is our present property system; the difference being only that one would not be entitled to the retention of the rents from such titles. On the other hand, since rents would be returned to the community, other tax regimes could be abolished.

The use of this fairly highbrow Georgian economic theory to convince uninitiated local decision makers to transform their tax regimes cannot be a simple task. I have struggled with a challenge at least remotely similar in recent years, working with the countries of East Europe transitioning from Marxian central planning regimes and Soviet-type economies to market-oriented democracy. The issue was encouraging the use of the property tax (conceptually a first step toward the use of a land-value tax) in the pursuit of fiscal decentralization. It would have been quite natural for subnational governments in those postcommunist countries to adopt a more serious property tax ideally suited to provide local governments with independent sources of revenue and much greater local autonomy (Bryson, 2010).

Ten years of rather intensive research in the Czech and Slovak Republics on this issue convinced me that matters of taxation, guided by parliaments and finance ministries, are not a fruitful field for the implementation of policies based on esoteric, theoretical considerations of economic optimality. The political pressures emanating from sources other than economic theory are much more real and pressing than Georgist considerations. Still, the Georgists persist in their efforts to spread the word. And it is a word very much worth spreading.

It is also worth noting here that in the Soviet transition from communism to market-based economic institutions, Georgists from the United Kingdom and the United States traveled to Russia nine times in the early 1990s to promote land value taxation. Fred Harrison was one of the delegation's leaders. He sent a letter to Gorbachev with the signatures of leading Western economists, including several Nobel laureates. (See http://www.cooperativeindividualism. org/dodson_mission_to_moscow.html and http://www. earthsharing.org.au/2006/09/15/letter-to-gorbachev/.)

George's Influence beyond the Community of Georgists

It has been shown that George has had an important influence on many in and beyond the scholarly community from his own time down to our day. Although he never lived to see it, his persuasive writings and teachings clearly had a major impact on the anti-trust movement of the early twentieth century and helped to rein in the monopolistic influences in the American economy of that era. The influence George had in other areas, on both the intellectual and political life of the country, was important. The influence he and his followers had on the political processes discussed in this chapter was, from my perspective, surprisingly strong rather than surprisingly weak. But, of course, my expectations are not Georgist.

Gaffney (1999) has offered another way of expressing this fact. He acknowledges that the case for reducing taxes on structures and for increasing the yield from taxes on land was made very clear in concept by Georgists long ago. Taxing real estate structures is a disincentive for the great work of development that produces buildings and other improvements located on the land. If effort and creativity are taxed, people will be inclined to invest less effort and creativity into their projects; people are more inclined to work for themselves than they are for their government. But if land or other natural resources, free gifts of nature, are taxed, the productive and creative effort of developing and using them will not be affected; moreover, the inclination to use them speculatively will be countered by the tax. It will become costly to withhold such lands from active use while waiting for the economic growth and development that will substantially increase their value.

This is all based, of course, on Ricardian rent theory, which recognizes that early on in the development of a village, town, or city, a cost-covering price will provide a market equilibrium. With the supply of land being fixed by nature and the demand dependent on the productivity of land and the size of the population, we have the conditions we need for Ricardian rent to arise.[31] With the growth of cities, land use expands to lands of lower productivity and of less desirable location (implying also higher transportation costs on many kinds of transactions). The rent accruing to the more favorable plots of land is not the result of greater productive efficiency or creativity on the part of the landholders involved. We have seen that it is due solely to the progress of the community and to the economies of scale and agglomeration associated with the development of cities. George wanted such rents to be taxed away and enjoyed by the whole community responsible for their creation. The land tax would also make it costly to hold land idle strictly for speculative gain, which would mean that such lands would be used sooner and more productively after the imposition of the tax. That, in turn, would cause more compact city development, reducing sprawl and transportation costs.

George's single tax notion would avoid taxing the buildings and structures in the most highly developed parts of cities, since they are the result of productive and creative effort, which should not be penalized with tax. Rather, only the value of the land itself would be subject to tax, thus capturing the land rent for the whole community. It will be argued that it is difficult, if not impossible, to determine the value of unique properties in downtown locations. Even active real estate markets fail to produce consistently prices of recently sold, comparable properties as a guide to the values of particular parcels of land available on the market.

But modern economists, sometimes under the influence and inspiration of Henry George, have done and are currently doing interesting work on such issues. Plassman and Tideman (2003) have provided insightful work on assessing the value of downtown land, which they separate into two parts; sales prices indicate real estate market values without separating the value of land and the improvements located on it. Their article presents an empirical method for determining the value of land *per se* and the separate value of structures on and improvements to the land.

This technical question, however, cannot be viewed as a final barrier to the implementation of George's single tax. Brown (1997a) reminds us that the fundamental policy issues George addressed some 130 years ago remain as pressing and as difficult to deal with today as they were then.

Essentially, we are forced today to ask the same question he struggled with. How do you find an equitable balance between the public's common interests in land and natural resources and the private property rights effective markets seek to protect?

Gaffney attributes society's failure to take advantage of the knowledge gained through George and his predecessors about society's use of the land and natural resources to the absence of "active, focused support" from those standing to gain from its implementation and "to the lack of understanding on the part of voters and policymakers" (Gaffney, 1999, p. 106).

At the time of writing this chapter, the only discussion on taxation in the United States, aside from the potential hazards of simply increasing most types already extant in response to massive government deficits, was on the potential adoption of a value-added tax (VAT) as a means to increase government revenues significantly. The question currently seems not to be the positive or negative characteristics of prospective forms of taxation, but only the size of potential revenue streams associated with given types of tax. Regrettably, our political representatives seem concerned with taxes only as a means of "getting at" the revenues they seek, apparently blissfully ignorant of the fact that different tax policies have different and powerful implications for our lives.

Although there are no political prospects for the adoption of a single tax in the United States or other countries today, Wasserman (2003) and other economists, including myself, would argue that the property tax (not likely to become a "single tax") should remain an important contributor to the financing of public services. Wasserman, like George, would argue moreover that the property tax should target the value of land rather than the productive enterprise and improvements on it. "Land-value taxation," enthusiastically discussed by many modern economists, few of whom could fairly be described as "Georgists," has already received wide application in policy affairs.

Consider some of the policy developments in the lands mentioned above as having been developed under Georgist influence. These include taxing the land at a higher rate than the associated improvements and structures; partial or even complete exemption of improvements; making up for lost revenues by increasing levies on the land; applying a surtax to properties of absentee ownership; and attempting to reduce speculation through a high rate of tax on the profits derived from land sales.

Conclusions

George's views on land use and land policy retain an important influence on contemporary life. Showing this provides a bridge to the final chapter of the book, which addresses George's influence on contemporary economics in general.

Economists favoring the use of a land tax, as opposed to that of a more typical real estate or property tax, propose *not* to tax improvements on land, but the land only. A recent discussion in the *National Tax Journal* on that issue was initiated with an article by England and Zhao (2005), which explored the shifting away from single-rate property taxation to a two-rate system in Dover, New Hampshire. They found this new tax, applying a lower rate to improvement values than to land values, is superior to a uniform rate tax yielding the same revenue. They found also that the revised tax would have a regressive impact, so they recommended a tax credit provision to offset the regressivity.

A later article (Bowman and Bell, 2008) reported that a similar investigation of Roanoke, Virginia, actually yielded results that were progressive rather than regressive for a tax applied to land rather than improvement (as in the England/Zhao study). The study concluded that the resulting tax change would be of greatest benefit for areas with the lowest incomes and greatest poverty rates. These studies demonstrate that the use of a land tax of the type George recommended remains a very relevant and timely issue today.

Since Charles Tiebout (1956) published a famous and frequently cited paper on public choice and local public finance, the issue of the property tax has been integral to the question of financing local governments. The Tiebout model is based on the need for a local tax that provides robust revenues but does not distort either the local economy's production or other local government revenue sources. As described by George, the land tax is clearly one that makes the Tiebout model work.

In the local public finance and fiscal decentralization literatures there is general consensus that the property tax should be assigned to subnational governments, since it has several attractive features when in place at that level.[32] First, it applies to an immobile base and its application will not affect other commodity and factor inputs. It is viewed as an efficient tax and it is relatively neutral with respect to revenue yields (i.e., it will have no affect on them) from important alternative sources of local government revenue.

Second, the property tax satisfies the benefit principle. Where land values are enhanced through the provision of local government services, for example, access to sewerage, drinking water, electricity and roads, such benefits are capitalized into the value of the land. Financing these public services through the property tax can bring incentive compatibilities into government services and contribute to local government efficiency.

Third, as a function of a plot's size, the value of a property may be related to the taxpayer's ability to pay the tax. So property tax burdens can be progressively distributed to assure greater fairness of the tax system. Finally, because the property tax is highly visible, it is conducive to enhancing accountability among subnational governments.

Other advantages of this form of taxation are their potential for providing substantial and stable revenues to local governments.

Unfortunately, there are a number of issues with the property tax which make it less attractive and less utilized than its abstract, positive qualities would suggest to be appropriate. One of the more significant problems is that this kind of tax is far from popular in many places, both among taxpayers and tax collectors. Assessments may seem arbitrary, the tax provides liquidity problems for homeowners with valuable real estate assets but only low incomes, and the visibility of the tax all work against its being popular. At the same time, it is expensive to administer with its necessary fiscal cadastre, its requirements for updating property assessments, and the necessity of collecting tax from reluctant and cash-strapped taxpayers. These problems are quite common in developing countries and those countries transitioning from a communist past. And they are certainly not unheard of in other countries as well.

George's influence on land policy has indeed been widespread and has resulted in policies demonstrative of what could be achieved with serious intent to install more optimal tax measures and land use. The Lincoln Institute of Land Policy in Boston, Massachusetts, has recognized this importance as it has worked to apply positive insights and policy suggestions in the spirit of George to the nation's land policy. It has also worked with organizations and governments around the world as a sort of organizational consultant on tax measures and land use policies. The institute indicates that in recent decades various tax jurisdictions have effectively used land taxes to recapture value created by the public sector. Especially in those countries recently transitioning from central planning regimes to democratic, market-oriented systems and those countries in the developing world, land taxes have proved to be an important source of revenue and have provided strong stimuli to economic development (Brown and Smolka, 1997b; Youngman and Malme, 2001).

It is often pointed out that George's single tax is in principle a good idea, but one which in the contemporary United States could not provide the huge amounts of funding required to run government as its scope increases. Many kinds of taxes are relied upon to provide the funds necessary to finance modern governments adorned with costly social programs. Nevertheless, in many countries governments could perform normal functions based on sustainable revenues, economic growth and poverty reduction that could be financed from an effective land tax.

The popular acceptance of a narrower tax on increments in land value, which represent returns to public investment, seems to be growing. The forms taken by these taxes "range from a direct tax on land value increments in Colombia to impact fees for residential developments in many parts of the United States" (Brown and Smolka, 1997b, p. 29). These authors foresee even wider use of such taxes in this new century.

It can be supposed that Henry George would object to the use of narrower, land-based taxes in lieu of his single tax system on all land value, but Brown and Smolka argue that the new approach does provide similar benefits. The ethical argument for capturing land rents from private owners and the publicly created value reflected in such rents, is as appropriate today as when Henry George advocated it. Other taxes capturing private gains produced by public investment represent an appealing modern application of single tax theory.

With these narrower land-based taxes there is concern about the fairness issue, since current voters in a local jurisdiction can impose taxes on taxpayers who have not yet arrived to exercise their franchise. It needs to be shown that local political power can be balanced with the desire of the community to capture value created by community effort.

Substituting a land-based tax for currently extant taxes to pay for public investment represents economic efficiency. Taxes on other resources, physical structures or labor, for example, affect market incentives and tend to distort decision making. A land tax is absorbed by the landowner and, because the land is immobile, the tax does not cause the landowner to take his land to a neighboring state nor does it reduce the inherent incentives and efficiency of use.

Just as George taught, land-based taxes force land prices down and remove the possibility of holding land idle without cost for the purpose of speculation. Since land prices are surging in many locations globally, downward pressure on prices represents a benefit to national economies, and especially to their lower-income households. Finally, although it is unlikely that land tax revenues could cover all public expenditures in modern economies, they could at least pay for a significant part of public infrastructure investment and provide significant support for local budgets.

Granted, the contemporary information economy has changed greatly from the developing, agricultural economy of Henry George's day. Thus, the land policies implied by his classical brand of economics may seem to be an historical anachronism. But the basic theory still applies and the conceptual equity and efficiency advantages of a land tax remain highly relevant. This is the reason Henry George's economics have been successfully applied on several continents and in numerous locations. Many of George's conclusions still hold. They remind us that George's analysis was insightful and productive of important policy conclusions. It is of worth to review that analysis and discover the lessons that still apply in today's world; in doing so, we come again to the realization that Henry George was probably the greatest early American economist. We also recognize why history has tended to rehabilitate George's work and are prepared to appreciate the next and final chapter of this book, which addresses his influence on contemporary economics in general.

Appendix: Georgist Publications and Online Literature

Part I: Nobel Laureates Who Have Endorsed Henry George's Work

The Georgists are scarcely just zealots with an oversized pre-occupation with Henry George. Every committed Georgist is in some manner the result of an intellectual encounter with the scholarly ideas of George. Many are men and women of scholarship and affairs. Some are active in promoting the fundamental ideas of the single tax in their communities and countries. An impressive number are academic economists and social scientists whose scholarly work often reflects George's theories.

Georgists are often allied with the world's most distinguished economists. Because George's economics are as sound as Adam Smith's or David Ricardo's, his writings have been endorsed by many economists. A series of quotes by Nobel Laureates is representative of the views of the academy today. It would have been impossible in George's own time to have found such endorsements, given the prejudices of the classical and neoclassical economists of his day. But history has rehabilitated George's work.

The site of the Henry George Foundation of America, listed below, displays the names of endorsers Milton Friedman, Herbert Simon, Paul Samuelson, James Tobin, James Buchanen, Franco Modigliani, Robert Solow, and William Vickrey. James Mirlees and Joseph Stiglitz have recently been added to that number. It would be difficult to find a list of any other Nobel winners whose writings and works are more widely known than those of these distinguished individuals.

The fundamental ideas that arise from the endorsements of these Nobel Prize winners relate to the following principles:

- Taxes should be on land (and natural resources) rather than on improvements, that is, the single tax or land value tax idea.
- The tax burden on the people would be reduced by a land tax rather than a wage or an income tax, combined with other forms of taxation.
- The tax on land rent provides wealth for the community that does not distort production incentives or efficiency.
- The user of land should be taxed on an annual basis by the local government, not on a one-time-only basis. The tax should be the current rental value of the land that the owner prevents others from using.
- With the single tax no landowners dispossess their fellow citizens by obtaining a disproportionate share of the natural resources (especially land) that nature provides for humanity.

Part II: Contemporary Georgists and Their Activities and Projects

Below is a list of some of the most important websites that reveal the important ideas and efforts of the Georgists and of the organizations supportive of the application of George's ideas.

http://www.cgocouncil.org/
This site of the Council of Georgist Organizations supplies a long list of Georgist organizations, institutes, and schools with contact data for each. Information on the annual conference of this umbrella organization is also posted.

http://schalkenbach.org/
The Robert Schalkenbach Foundation, based in New York, promotes Henry George's work largely through its publications program and through distribution of the materials with an online library and an online bookstore. George's works, especially *Progress and Poverty*, are featured.

http://www.lincolninst.edu/aboutlincoln/
The Lincoln Institute came into being because of John C. Lincoln's devotion to Henry George's work. Over time the focus changed to the chosen areas of study of the institute as expressed at the Institute's website: Planning and Urban Form; Valuation and Taxation; and International Studies. Much good modern work in these areas has been performed by the Institute. Although none of the tabs on the home page provide rubrics about Henry George himself, typing his name into the search bar turns up some very good sources on George and on the relationship of the Institute's work to his.

http://www.cooperativeindividualism.org/heroes.html
This site of the School of Cooperative Individualism, designed to promote a just society, features a page on Henry George, which provides a lot of information presented and organized by Ed Dodson on George's life and works. Included are a wealth of quotes of many famous persons whose comments reveal deep admiration for George's work. For example, although quotes of Nobel laureates are favorites of the Georgists, this site quotes Nobel laureate Gary Becker of the University of Chicago as saying: "the first book I looked at in economics was Progress and Poverty. It's a wonderful book and had a lasting impact on me" (in a speech at St. John's University, April 23, 1992).

http://www.wealthandwant.com/auth/Batt.html
The website "Wealth and Want" provides a rich collection of articles and abstracts on very contemporary issues

and applications to urban life that reflect the theories and philosophies of Henry George.

http://www.answersanswers.com/land_rent_examples.html
Various places that have undertaken to install some variant of a land value tax as an experiment are listed and discussed here. Also, statements of famous economists and some of history's most famous personalities are presented on the single tax.

http://www.taxreform.com.au/economists.php
The full quotes of most of the Nobel Laureates endorsing Henry George are presented on this Australian site.

http://ourcommonwealth.org/about-us/8-nobel-laureates-in-economics-have-endorsed-a-tax-on-land-rather-than-on-production

This site of the Henry George Foundation of America tracks the policy reform efforts of Georgists in Pennsylvania and other states. It also displays a list of Nobel Laureates who have endorsed Henry George's ideas and economics principles.

CHAPTER 6

Henry George and Modern Economics

Introduction

There was a time when Henry George was not merely one of the most widely read American economists, he was also one of the country's most widely read authors in general. Many of his contemporary economists would have been inclined to consider him a political journalist rather than an economist. His most famous work, *Progress and Poverty*, had gained a wide, general readership both in and beyond the United States,[1] although it was a scholarly work more serious than today's trade books written by economists *cum* political commentators.

Today, when even economists are no longer systematically trained in the history of their discipline, as they were in the graduate programs of my era, young economists often have no idea who Henry George might have been. That, of course, is not surprising. This great writer attended no university and his only instructors were the antiquarian volumes of already defunct classical economists.

As we saw in an earlier chapter, George was writing his classical treatise at a time when Alfred Marshall and other great minds were busy on both sides of the Atlantic developing a new approach to economic analysis—neoclassical theory. It was designed to replace the work of Henry George (along with that of all other classical economists) almost before it was published. But these theoretical architects could not totally free themselves from the influences of George's theory, so popular and persuasive to many at the time. Stabile (1995) shows us, for example, George's influence on the famous American economist, John Bates Clark.

Some economists of the Georgist persuasion, however, find George's influence on the profession of his day much more profound than we would infer, for example, from Stabile. It is more profound than the number of George's books sold or the number of people outside academia who were adherents of his economic theory. Gaffney and Harrison (1994), appreciated that Henry George and his proposed reforms presented a serious threat to the landed and academic interests of his time. Now, many decades later, even most economists are generally uninformed as to the degree that the development of modern, Neoclassical economics was distorted, pushed off its development path, because of a direct effort to thwart and discredit George's theories. The express purpose was to discomfit his followers and reprogram future students who might be unduly influenced by his arguments.

These authors anticipate the reaction most of us in the profession can be expected to have when confronted with these assertions. They concede that George seems too minor a figure historically to justify the efforts of early neoclassicists to refute with such vehemence. That impression demonstrates the degree to which the discrediting efforts of the neoclassicals were achieved. He has become in general, for those who know of George at all, what the academics sought to make of him. It took them a whole generation, Gaffney and Harrison point out, but by 1930 they had essentially robbed George of his stature. While succeeding in doing so, however,

> they emasculated the discipline, impoverished economic thought, muddled the minds of countless students,

rationalized free-riding by landowners, took dignity from labor, rationalized chronic unemployment, hobbled us with today's counterproductive tax tangle, marginalized the obvious alternative system of public finance, shattered our sense of community, subverted a rising economic democracy for the benefit of rent-takers, and led us into becoming an increasingly nasty and dangerously divided plutocracy.

(pp. 30, 31)

By way of contrast, according to this view, George synthesized a plan combining the better characteristics and discarding the less admirable features of collectivism and individualism. His work was passionate, articulate and persuasive, allowing him to win advocates among the laboring classes as well as among the intelligentsia. There were sincere and serious attempts by his followers to apply the policy prescriptions of *Progress and Poverty*.

John Maynard Keynes once made a statement of considerable appeal to economists when he said the deeds of policymakers are often influenced by the thought of already defunct economists. We have previously seen some of the impact that Henry George had on the economics profession of his time. In this chapter, the objective is to consider the influence that he has had on today's economics. We are asking the complex question as to whether the theories and doctrines economists learn, teach, and apply in the present retain any influence at all from George's writings.

To search for the spiritual ancestry of contemporary ideas is a treacherous undertaking. The sympathetic author may be inclined to see in writings addressed to an earlier generation hints of insights valued as nuggets of intellectual gold. An old master, encountering a problem that had not yet been carefully analyzed, might make some offhand remark as to how that problem affected a topic under investigation. The remark may lead to an inference on the part of the sympathetic, contemporary reader suggesting that the old master had already thoroughly grasped the issue. Voila! We have discovered that current analysis was already a part of the toolkit of an earlier generation. But lacking the admiration inspiring the contemporary analyst, more dispassionate eyes simply cannot confirm that an obscure statement really was the insight that contained or at least led to the later development of a powerful new analysis.

An unrealistic evaluation can also run in the opposite direction. One may fail fully to appreciate the maturity of economists of previous generations. These individuals were endowed with less powerful statistical and mathematical tools for their analyses, but after decades of observation and contemplation were often able to achieve powerful insights into economic phenomena. We might observe that he who fails to learn from past errors after decades of observation of the effects of economic policy is condemned to repeat them.

One is reminded in considering these principles of the recent financial crisis. Before the financial crisis of 2007 the world was in awe of the financial "techies" of Wall Street. They were capable of generating financial instruments that dazzled the standard financial agent and permitted the impossible to be done—the "spreading" of risk over many investors, so that such risk could be discounted, if not completely ignored. Thus, assets that appeared to be terribly questionable were suddenly rendered marketable and capable of producing considerable profits. High-powered econometric tests assured those capable of understanding the complex models that all was well on Wall Street. Yet some of the most fundamental considerations never made it into the models. It became clear after the collapse of the financial universe that there had been something lacking in the financial models and in the wizardry of the techies (Bryson, 2010, chapter 12). Doubtless, financial analysts are now enjoying a return to the situation of the status quo ante in which they will again command larger salaries than nuclear physicists or brain surgeons, even before the crisis trauma has been overcome to a degree that recommends the full redeployment of our financial system's intellectual resources. But this is not the only example of learning (or failing to learn) from economic experience. After the onset of the global recession that followed the credit crisis, we worried about a recurrence of the great depression. So we rediscovered John Maynard Keynes and (to use a more modern term that may have been the only creative aspect of the refurbished policy) "economic stimulus," which became the order of the day. Whether or not incremental levels of government spending produce a multiplier effect on the gross domestic product depends, according to Keynesian theory, on the multipliers. When policymakers turned in 2007 and 2008 to this theory, which had largely been abandoned through the experiences of the 1960s and 1970s, few questions were asked about the multipliers, although Robert Barro (2009) warned that we could *not* expect their impacts to be considerable given the particulars of our historical situation. Actually experiencing and observing such a financial crisis and the resulting recession might prove to be more beneficial for young economists than a few extra years of pure academic pedagogy and reasoning. But that might only hold if they were to do so free from the biases promoted by the "financial technologies".

Like many other gifted economists, George's powers of observation and analysis grew through experience. George read, traveled, spoke, and wrote a great deal. He gained some helpful insights with the passage of his years. Because many of the phenomena that seem so new to each generation have also troubled the analysts of earlier times, it is worthwhile to investigate particular areas of research in which Henry George may have had some seminal insights.

Fortunately, in our investigation of this issue we are not alone. There are enough modern economists who are not only aware of George, but who have also produced a significant literature evaluating and analyzing his writings. There are enough of them producing sufficiently high-quality work that others, who are not intellectual fans of George, interact with them. Competent analysts are called upon through conferences or refereeing assignments to produce serious evaluations of the writings of George's admirers. So the question as to George's influence on modern economics has already produced a competent and interesting discussion as to George's value and contemporary influence. Even the writers who admire George, like those who are completely without any sentiments of advocacy in George's favor, are not generally inclined to think of themselves as the "Georgists" discussed in the previous chapter. But both of these groups are willing to give credit where credit is due, are unwilling to give it where it is not, and are not under the effects of the bias that seems to have colored much of the analysis of George's often envious and suspicious contemporaries.

This is, of course, a favorable situation for the present author. I need not be viewed as a biased reporter, even though I am an admirer of much of what Henry George stood for. I know the contemporary profession with its great strengths and occasional foibles, as well as some of the history of the profession that affected the scholarly outcomes and perceptions of George's day. But I need not try to convince the reader of any contemporary influence George might have today from the power of my own perceptions of the writings. I will simply report what others are writing and give my straightforward impressions as to the meaning of that part of the total literature that is to be reviewed here. I need not claim to be the discoverer of George in modern economics; I merely report what the discoverers are reporting.

In this chapter, let us first discuss George's thoughts on American capitalism in general. We shall review in that discussion George's views on issues of what later became the study of comparative economic systems. In considering his view of the economy's increasing complexity over time and the consequent movement toward socialism, we will see how his views compare with positions taken in modern comparative systems theories and how his view of the government compares with more contemporary views. Doing so will make it clear, hopefully, that George was not simply a socialist because he advocated confiscation of private lands. Some have had such a simplistic and inaccurate view of George's work, so it is helpful to dispel the notion that George's position on property rights in land (he did not advocate confiscation) made him in some fashion a socialist.

We will then turn to other areas of economics that have been influenced by Henry George. In spite of the growing literature regarding George's influence, Dwyer (1982) could write nearly 30 years ago that George's influence had been neglected in spite of the fact that he was read and discussed by Clark, Marshall, Hobson, Commons, Lerner, and Böhm-Bawerk.

Clark acknowledged the important stimulus of George on the development of his theory of marginal productivity. Dwyer credited George with having positively influenced "the neoclassical concept of capital, the theory of externality, the neoclassical versus the classical concept of monopoly; the entitlements approach to distributive justice; the burden of debt and other transfer incomes and capital formation and the theory of expectations." We will turn to some of the theories George helped develop after we have considered his view of the economic system of capitalism.

Henry George and the Economic System

The economic system consists of a resource allocation mechanism, which interacts with prevailing national financial, political and even cultural institutions. The prevailing resource allocation mechanism in the United States, the free market, finds expression through the general freedom and willingness of individual agents to buy and sell at prices on which they agree. George taught that the price mechanism would provide appropriate returns to the factors of production, determining the wages of labor, the interest of capital, and the rent of land as these factors are mobilized by the price mechanism (Pollard, 1979).

He discussed some of the important institutions in presenting the basic economic analysis of *Progress and Poverty*, but also addressed systemic issues in other writings. Some important insights are gleaned from *Social Problems* (George, 1883). Here, he wrote that if the purpose of government is to "secure the natural rights and equal liberty of the individual," the government must do for the mass of individuals "those things which cannot be done, or cannot be so well done, by individual action" (ibid., p. 158). This, of course, implies the traditional market-complementary activities of enforcing business law, regulating commerce and providing essential infrastructure. But it also opens the door to more extensive government participation in economic life.

George saw benefits in having the public budget include health, education and even recreation, as well as in providing "public encouragement" of science and invention. It was common in George's day for people to seek desirable services through voluntary cooperative societies and private action. George saw the potential, "if we can simplify and purify government," for society to obtain "in many other ways" and "in much larger degree" those same services. Moreover, they would be obtained with "the most enormous economies" (George, 1883, p. 170).

The sentiments expressed in this passage are certainly unusual for George. He seems here temporarily to forget some of his sharp criticisms of the government, for example, the egregious manner in which Congress ceded huge land grants to the railroads, then permitted monopolies in land ownership to develop, strengthening the foundations of poverty even more than those of progress. Ignoring the lack of confidence he was generally wont to express in the nation's policymakers, he even surmised that the simplified and puri-fied government of his mental lapse would be in a position to check a "growing tendency to adulteration and dishonesty," largely because such government could "reduce the appro-priative power of aggregated capital." He concluded with the observation that "the natural progress of social develop-ment is unmistakably toward cooperation, or, if the word be preferred, toward socialism, though I dislike to use a word to which such various and vague meanings are attached" (George, 1883, p. 170).

He wrote the following passage with an eye to the future rather than to the past:

> As in the development of species, the power of conscious, coordinated action of the whole being must assume greater and greater relative importance to the automatic action of parts, so is it in the development of society. This is the truth in socialism, which, although it is being forced upon us by industrial progress and social development, we are so slow to recognize.
>
> (ibid., p. 158)

The natural, cooperative proclivities of social arrangements and the need for governmental encouragement of education, science and research all suggest to George that socialism must be considered part of our future. George must be forgiven for having failed to live through the economic experiment of the Soviet Union and other European exper-iments, all of which have been calling for reform with growing insistence for the last quarter century or so. More-over, this temptation to liberal public service provision did not imply in George an instinct toward the kind of govern-ment control of economic production characteristic of the central planning that Stalin had not yet produced.

He hastened in these passages to emphasize that it is not government's business "to direct the employment of labor and capital, and to foster certain industries at the expense of other industries; and the attempt to do so leads to all the waste, loss and corruption due to protective tariffs" (ibid., p. 159). But George also conceded that there was a strong argument for government to expand its influence in private commerce in particular areas. It was that experience teaches that "any considerable interest having necessary relations with government is more corruptive of government when acting upon government from without than when assumed by government" (George, 1883, p. 165). As he observed the way the departments of government contracted for work and supplies and the corruption of the process, he concluded that direct employment would involve less corruption than contracting did, since it involved "a much greater concentration of corruptive interests and power" (ibid., p. 166). I believe this demonstrates that, even with his reasonably generous endowment of suspicion toward government policy, he was not as disillusioned with rent-seeking behavior, bureaucratic inefficiency and opportunism as the modern economists whose work will require additional reference below.

But George returns to the earlier caveat by explaining that his objective is

> to show that the simplification and purification of government are rendered the more necessary, on account of functions which industrial development is forcing upon government, and the further functions which it is becoming more and more evident that it would be advantageous for government to assume.
>
> (ibid., p. 171)

He also speaks of government without reference to the particular local, regional, national or supranational designation that would apply today. Of course in this chapter and elsewhere in speaking of government, the state, the community, et cetera, I use these terms in a general sense, without reference to existing political divisions. He found there was still need for considerable thought before addressing the proper organization of government, the distribution of powers and how they should evolve with the development of society (ibid., p. 172).

His conclusion to this question of governance was both stirring and constant to the message of the single tax. "There is no escape from it. If we would save the Republic before social inequality and political demoralization" have placed it beyond redemption, "we must assert the principle of the Declaration of Independence, acknowledge the equal and unalienable rights which inhere in man by endowment of the Creator, and make land common property" (ibid., p. 181).

He continued to maintain that public ownership of land is not necessary for the improvement and proper use of land. For that, we must merely secure the assurance that any labor and capital expended upon it would also in fact enjoy the reward for the expense. That can be accomplished through leasing land, as previous experience had made abundantly clear.

In any case, the truth cannot be misconstrued; George never advocated the confiscation of private property rights from landowners. As he often did, he stated unequivocally here that "it is not necessary, in order to secure equal rights to land, to make an equal division of land. All that it is necessary to do is to collect the ground-rents for the common benefit" (ibid., p. 185).

This is easily accomplished through taxation alone. One simply abolishes "all other forms of taxation until the weight of taxation rests upon the value of land irrespective of improvements, and take the ground-rent for the public benefit" (ibid., p. 185). In case it did not occur to the reader, George reminded that the abolition of all other taxes would greatly reduce the institutional costs of an "army" of tax officials, including accountants, collectors, assessors, spies, detectives and other government officials for customs, sales tax, and the personal and corporate tax departments. Moreover, the corrupting effect of indirect taxation would also disappear.

An excellent summary of George's work by Andelson (1994), which has been reproduced as the appendix to this chapter, makes some points that provide an appropriate conclusion to this section. Andelson illuminates George's view of capitalism effectively by noting that George thought of himself as a "purifier of capital" rather than as its adversary. Obviously, since he built upon the foundations of the classical economists, his system had a capitalist skeleton. Karl Marx referred to George's teaching as "Capitalism's last ditch," and George would have had to plead guilty to a firm belief in free markets, competition and in an unconstrained functioning of the laws of supply and demand. We have already observed his distrust of government and Andelson adds that he "despised" bureaucracy. He never considered the leveling of incomes an appropriate goal; the only appropriate equality was equal freedom of opportunity. If free enterprise could be freed of the monopolistic shackles preventing its effective operation, enterprise would truly be free.

George, somewhat like Joseph Schumpeter, had felt that there may be a certain inevitability in the forward march of socialism, as we have just observed. But when George penned a book addressed to the world's Catholics (George, 1894), "designed to draw a line between us and the socialists," we received further confirmation of his insistence that he was not in the socialist camp:

We differ from the Socialists in our diagnosis of the evil, and we differ from them in remedies. We have no fear of capital, regarding it as the natural handmaiden of labor; we look on interest in itself as natural and just; we would set no limit to accumulation, nor impose on the rich any burden that is not equally placed on the poor; we see no evil in competition, but deem unrestricted competition to be as necessary to the health of the industrial and social organism as the free circulation of the blood is to the bodily organism — to be the agency whereby the fullest cooperation is to be secured.

According to Andelson, George took only two conceptual items from the socialist menu of doctrines, but they were significant and strategic doctrines. First, each individual comes into the world with equal right of access to nature's bounties. Second, the community has a right to take that which it produces. But Andelson quickly reclaims these doctrines as originally having been Capitalist doctrines, as presented by John Locke, the Physiocrats, and Adam Smith. Since capitalist writers then basically ignored these conceptual positions, it was George's intent to rescue them from obscurity for good use in restoring balance and proportion to Capitalist doctrine.

Let the conclusion of this section defer to the words of George himself with respect to his view of the relationship between his single tax doctrine and his religious views, as expressed in *The Condition of Labor* (1894). Here he addresses the Pope and tells him that his own view of capitalism is as a living, organic mechanism moving forward in harmony with the divine, providing justice and freedom:

> But the fundamental difference — the difference I ask your Holiness specially to note — is in this: Socialism in all its phases looks on the evils of our civilization as springing from the inadequacy or in harmony of natural relations, which must be artificially organized or improved. In its idea there devolves on the State the necessity of intelligently organizing the industrial relations of men — the construction, as it were, of a great machine whose complicated parts shall properly work together under the direction of human intelligence. This is the reason why Socialism tends towards Atheism. Failing to see the order and symmetry of natural law, it fails to recognize God.

On the other hand, we who call ourselves single-tax men (a name which expresses merely our practical propositions) see in the social and industrial relations of men not a machine which requires construction, but an organism which needs only to be suffered to grow. We see in the natural, social, and industrial laws such harmony as we see in the adjustments of the human body, and that as far transcends the power of man's intelligence to order and direct as it is beyond man's intelligence to order and direct the vital movements of his frame. We see in these social and industrial laws so close a relation to the moral law as must spring from the same Authorship, and that proves the moral law to be the sure guide of man where his intelligence would wander and go astray. Thus, to us, all that is needed to remedy the evils of our time is to do justice and give freedom. This is the reason why our beliefs tend towards—nay, are indeed—the only beliefs consistent with a firm and reverent faith in God, and with the recognition of His law as the supreme law which men must follow if they would secure prosperity and avoid destruction. This is the reason why, to us, Political Economy only serves to show the depths of wisdom in the simple truths which common people heard gladly from the lips of Him of whom it was said with wonder, "Is not this the Carpenter of Nazareth?"

Henry George and Contemporary Fields of Specialization in Economics

A good place to begin a discussion of George's influence on today's fields of specialization in economics is with the Lincoln Institute of Land Policy in Boston, Massachusetts, which was organized to honor Henry George's memory through the practical application of his contributions to economics. The institute has been credited by a Nobel laureate, Robert M. Solow (1997), with having kept George's ideas alive and effective by developing and refining them, even by extending them to issues of land use, urban reform, and taxation in ways that Solow assures us could never have crossed George's mind.

Urban Economics, Urban Development and Urban Renewal

The very title of this section suggests several rather specialized research directions branching out from George's interest in the use of land and the implications of the single tax suggestion for land use. Clearly, scholars interested in these topics would often have an interest in the role they play in an urban setting. The work of the Lincoln Land Institute is directly focused on these fields and the Institute has an ambitious research agenda productive of many publications. Their work is richly complemented by active work with the academic institutions of numerous countries.

The Nobel laureate William Vickrey, whose work in the areas of taxation and land policy ranged from very clever to profoundly creative (Vickrey, 1999, for example), supplied many contributions to the area under discussion. In 1977 he published a paper comparing cities to firms, the latter being seen by economists as the source of society's productivity and as the object of theories on market models. To Vickrey it was important to see the city as having the possibility of being so organized in the public services that it produces as to achieve the kind of efficient operation that firms do under competitive conditions.

Cities exist, Vickrey (2001) postulated, because of productive activities combining population density (offering labor supplies) with economies of scale. People congregate in dense settlements to produce where capital has been accumulated to permit production costs to decline as the volume of output increases. Transportation costs provide incentive for such concentrations of the factors of production.

Efficient allocation of resources in decentralized cities will be achieved when the pricing of all goods and services, including public services, is efficient. For the private market in which firms participate, that requires that marginal cost and marginal revenues are at equality. For the city as firm (Vickrey, 1977), it is necessary that public services are produced at short-run marginal social cost, which means that social costs and benefits external to the production costs of public services are also taken into account.

It is also important to note Vickrey's caveat that where economies of scale (declining production costs for increasingly large outputs) exist for activities of the city, setting prices at the level of marginal social cost will not produce revenues that cover total costs. In that case a subsidy will be required to push output to the level that will take full advantage of scale economies. And where should these public funds come from?

The answer was simple for a brilliant contemporary economist not indoctrinated, as he might have been a century earlier, against the very sound work of Henry George. Vickrey proposed that the subsidy should be covered by taxing urban lands, that is, site values. The subsidies that would make possible marginal cost pricing for public services would efficiently and equitably be provided by the tax on site values.

Mispricing public services by failure to follow this rule would reduce urbanization's potential benefits. In practice, of course, the pricing of urban public services is generally distorted as the rule is observed more in the breach. Vickrey provided creative ideas on the appropriate application of marginal cost pricing and the benefits that such would entail. Site value taxation is an old idea, having been rediscovered by Henry George. It is a part of the contemporary property tax and is, as we have seen, the good part. It is the part that is non-distortionary and is not so regressive as some other forms of taxation. The other part of the property tax is one of the worst kinds of tax, the tax on buildings and structures. This part discourages investment and distorts economic activity as we have seen in earlier chapters.

Gaffney (2001) has also elaborated on George's prescient, yet also simply historical view of the correct approach to urban lands. George saw cities as locations for communication, cooperation, and exchange; they were for him the basis of civilization and a possibility for new frontiers based on the increasing returns generated by their synergies. Modern considerations of the economics of agglomeration are also an interesting facet of the studies of urban economics.

Multivariate interactions of economic agents associating as active market participants can be synergistic in the urban setting. Each parcel of land is developed in the stage of decreasing returns, but the composite city is generally in a stage of increasing returns due to those synergies.

Agglomeration economies are an inherent part of healthy growth and are the substance of urban economics (Arnott, 2004). They are the result of the location of firms in geographic and economic proximity with the opportunity for positive, productive interaction involving economies of scale and network effects. The clustering of these firms in urban areas permits declining production costs through greater specialization and division of labor. It is further enhanced as multiple suppliers compete for business.

The productivity of the whole provides greater yields than the sum of the growth of the parts. George understood, according to Gaffney (2001), the key phenomenon of his time, which was overlooked by his contemporaries. It was simply that this synergistic surplus lodges in the rents of urban lands, giving rise to the increase of urban rents and land prices that endowed landowners with wealth and power. He who fails to understand ground rents and land prices fails to understand cities. Those ground rents continue to accrue in perpetuity and generally tend to rise. If the ground rents are taxed, a whole range of social dividends is produced in the cause of both equity and efficiency. Urban renewal is also promoted because taxing the ground rents permits reduction or even complete elimination of taxation on buildings and structures. It is a stimulus to construction as it assures greater liquidity for developers of new buildings. It increases productivity in surrounding regions as the synergies spread. It encourages owner occupancy and efficient land use, stimulates the formation of capital and discourages governmental corruption. In short, Gaffney shows how the single tax solution to the problems of economic development can be realized in a contemporary urban setting.

In addressing the question of optimal city size, Arnott refers to the Henry George Theorem, which avers that efficiently organized economic activity over a large space will result in an equality of aggregate land rents and aggregate losses incurred from activities with decreasing returns to scale. The Henry George Theorem has been used to investigate, for example, whether the population of Tokyo is larger than optimal for economic purposes. Arnott's (1979) research has sought to determine the generality of the Theorem and whether it is a conceptually productive method for estimating whether cities are overpopulated or of less than optimal population size. He concludes that the Theorem is not well-suited to assist in determining the optimal size of cities, although it holds in a general sense.

An alternative form of the theorem hypothesizes that a city of identical individuals of optimal numbers will produce an equality of expenditure on pure local public goods and differential land rents. Pure local public goods (and services) benefit all citizens equally without excluding any of the population. Differential land rents are simply the aggregate of urban land rent in the city minus the opportunity cost of land in nonurban use. Where these conditions actually hold, we would expect Henry George's single tax, appropriately confiscating the land rents, would be sufficient on its own to finance appropriate public expenditures for the city. In such a city, the optimal city size is determined by two opposing actions. As the city's population grows, the fixed cost of pure local public goods are spread over larger numbers of citizens, providing increasing returns to scale in the city and promoting economic agglomeration.

But as the city population grows and spreads, the marginal travel costs associated with production increase. This source of decreasing returns to scale encourages a spatial dispersion of economic activity. In short, when the population size is optimal, increasing returns to scale arising from local public goods just offset decreasing returns to scale arising from land scarcity.

Where the city's populace consists of heterogeneous rather than identical people, endowed with differing characteristics of taste and productivity, the optimal population size is more difficult to specify. Here, the Henry George Theorem specifies that Pareto optimal allocation expenditures on pure local public goods will tend toward equality with differential land rents.

Holcombe (2004) has elaborated on the reasons why these interesting ideas are insufficient to establish rigorously what the optimal size of a city might be. A very basic problem is that agglomeration economies have nothing to do with local public goods. Numerous other problems suggested by Holcombe also demonstrate the impossibility of using the Henry George Theorem to solve the riddle of optimal city size.

The final issue in urban economics relates to the land use theories of Henry George and the modern concept of the "winner's curse." Tideman (2004) points out that George's theory of land speculation was inconsistent with the modern assumption that economic actors perform their functions on the basis of perfect knowledge. But it is consistent with the recently developed theory of the winner's curse (Milgrom and Weber, 1982).

Henry George claimed two especially important virtues for the land tax. First, as observed by Adam Smith and the physiocrats long ago, land taxes do not inhibit production as other taxes do. Second, they eliminate land speculation. With the single tax, there would no longer be an inclination to hold land out of production on the basis of expectations that the prices of land would continue to rise. All land would be made available for development and improvement and land prices would fall as land monopolization ceased to be profitable.

In communities enjoying rapid progress, steady increases of land rents are built into expectations; the margin of cultivation, George taught, will extend beyond that required by the necessities of production. This is observed in every rapidly growing city. Some of the lands of superior quality are withheld from use, forcing a premature employment of inferior quality lands in production, scattering vacant lots across the uneven development of the community and leaving "miserable shanties in the midst of costly buildings." Both the vacant land and the shanties represent owners waiting for further price rises before giving their land up to development. Their action drives economic activity at the limits of the city much further away from the city center.

This theory of speculation should not be evaluated in terms of modern theory assuming perfect foresight. Rather, it represents an alternative theory that maximizes expected utility under uncertainty. Actions taken here may be based on imperfect or incomplete knowledge and lead to the infamous "winner's curse" of Milgrom and Weber. An analysis of the implication of actions taken by individuals motivated by differing mistaken beliefs gave rise to the insight of the curse. When people of divergent valuations of an item or event of uncertain value compete or bid for that item or event, the highest bidder will be the one who made the greatest error in the overestimation of its value. Auction participants, for example, who are aware of this persistent phenomenon, should lower their bids in light of the uncertainty so as not to incur significant losses should they succeed in their bid.

Ironically, such individuals can be expected not to moderate their bids to levels that would yield positive returns on their action.

Tideman's application of this principle to land speculation is appropriate since the future value of land is uncertain. The highest bidder will be the one who has most seriously overestimated the future value of the land. Those who do overestimate its future value will certainly not pursue potentially profitable current uses of the land, opting instead for the greater, overestimated profits sought in speculation.

This creative approach of the winner's curse is not without its own difficulties, also discussed by Holcombe (2004), who finds that real estate markets are sufficiently different from auctions that the idea does not offer the promise hoped for. Moreover, Holcombe reminds us of the positive function played by leapfrogging. If there were absolutely smooth development of communities geographically, all new development would have to be at the periphery. Leapfrogging makes it possible for strategically located plots to be used for higher density commercial purposes, such as shopping malls, with the advantage of some centrality of location for highly desirable latecomer candidates in development.

In any case, it must be an irony particularly galling to both George and to Tideman, that to some degree, widespread land speculation often proves to be a self-fulfilling prophecy of higher prices resulting from speculation's artificially produced scarcity of land. The speculators seem almost to be engaged conspiratorially to constrict the supply of land and drive up prices. Creative thinking along these lines has offered some hints about where modern theory might go, even though in these cases the thoughts of Henry George working in the minds of his successors have not yet blossomed into spectacular new theories. Nevertheless, George's accomplishment[2] has been to produce many admirers who have extended his work into numerous individual contributions across several fields of economics and policy, another of which we turn to now.

Henry George and Rent-Seeking

William Baumol is another distinguished contemporary economist who has paid some attention to George's work. Baumol (2004, p. 9) finds three main messages in George's memorable work, *Progress and Poverty*. "First, that the rent of land is an egregious contributor to inequality; second, that rent, unlike other income sources, can be taxed without detrimental incentive effects; and third, that this is so because pure rent is a payment for which the recipient provides no production to society in return."

Baumol expresses his desire to update George's work. The work needs updating, he finds, because it deals with land, the basic resource or factor input of agriculture, which has shrunk continually since George's day. This has been a concomitant of agriculture's shrinking share of gross domestic product. The shrinkage has been, of course, as rapid as the expansion of the industry, services and information sectors of the economy. Baumol finds it difficult to understand why people could take interest in a topic which relates to a mere 2 percent of GDP, which is what payments for the rent of land represent today. He admits that George's analysis remains pertinent and important, but is much more so if it is generalized and its applicability is extended to include the contemporary scene, rather than just the situation of the later nineteenth century.

Economists focus on the third of George's above-mentioned observations, namely, that rent is a payment to a recipient who makes no contribution to national product. They have come to use the term "rent" in recent years to refer to any uncompensated payment. When monopolists, for example, enjoy large profits merely because they have restricted the industry's total output, economists consider the results of this perfidy "rent." Baumol finds it is rent precisely in this generalized sense that is at the "forefront of modern economic developments." In Baumol's view, it is the Enrons, the financial firms and other top corporate managements that have successfully provided themselves with "obscenely high incomes," in spite of presiding over firms of strikingly meager economic performance. These, he believes, are the contemporary counterparts of George's landholders.

Human capital (which Baumol might be more inclined to describe as entrepreneurial capital) has replaced land as the economy's most vital productive factor. People are willing to supply those endowed with abundant stocks of it with large rents. Interestingly, if people were required to pay a lump-sum tax on the estimated market value of their human capital holdings (for their college degree, for any graduate study, especially the MBA, and for any specialized training, internship, or informative experience, including important kinds of work experience over time), that tax would likely be as difficult to shift as a tax on land.[3]

Baumol finds that the entrepreneurial function in the Schumpeterian sense is the key factor in the dynamic growth of the U.S. economy over recent decades. So Baumol hastens on to discuss entrepreneurship, leaving Henry George mired in the less interesting land factor of a distant past. As Baumol uses George to talk about theories that have little relationship to George, this chapter has also used Baumol to introduce the notion of rent and rent-seeking as an important branch of modern economics that has been developed in the spirit of Henry George.

Borcherding et al. (1998) have explicitly called attention to the fact that George contributed important early insights into the phenomenon of the rent seeking of special interests. In their view, his insights were illustrative of what became, long after his time, public choice analysis, also borrowed by political scientists and sociologists for their own purposes as "rational choice theory." These authors see in George's devotion to the study of political economy, which was already starting to slip from fashion among academic economists in George's own day, the evidence that he was among the first of the public choice analysts. His intense interest in and frequent analysis of policy issues reflected his conviction about the importance of incentives in the behavior and decisions of economic agents. Borcherding et al. cite his remark that "political economy, fearlessly pursued, must lead to conclusions that will be as a lion in the way to those who have any tenderness for 'vested interests' " (George, 1886, p. 9).

By discussing advisable limitations on the role of government and the likelihood of intragovernmental corruption, George, almost single-handedly in the nineteenth century, outlined the modern theory of rent seeking.[4]

Although the terms "rent seeking," and "public choice" were not the ones George used in his writings, he used the concepts long before others began to do so. The notion was not strange to classical economics, but it was lost during the era of the marginal revolution. Gordon Tullock (1967) and Anne Krueger (1974), reintroduced and developed the analysis that has become so widely discussed today. Fundamental principles are that the state blocks free markets and by permitting, even encouraging, redistribution in the interest of special interest groups, it diminishes the general welfare as a whole. Furthermore, unproductive rent-seeking activities burden investment and reduce the capital stock and future growth. Rent-seeking thus gives rise to market failure by political means. George himself used the example of the raising of an army to illustrate the development of inefficient rent-seeking behavior.

Henry George and Economic Development

Henry George's influence on development economics needs at least brief mention. Third world economies, usually attempting to make their way to modernity through what resources they have available, must be particularly interested in agriculture and land. For the same reasons that the more developed economies can benefit from incentive-compatible forms of taxation, the more fortunate developing countries will inevitably discover this need.

Backhaus (2004), Lewis (1985), and the Nobel laureate Joseph Stiglitz (2003) have addressed the beneficial effects of considering what Henry George taught about the single tax on land for the developing world. Backhaus holds, correctly in my view, that sustainable growth is the result of judicious use of natural resources, no less for the developing countries than for those more advanced. The tax system is of extreme importance to the use of land and natural resources. Often, the legal system, inevitably a product of the level of development, proves to be a hindrance in developing the structure and instruments available for the tax system and fails adequately to regulate the use of natural resources in the required manner. It will usually be unsuited as well to provide for the necessary diversity for internationally competitive economic activity.

Stiglitz discusses some of the basic principles taught by Henry George as they apply in developing countries, also anticipating the same effects that George postulated. They center on the positive effects we expect from applying a tax to land rather than the structures on the land, the incomes of the individual or corporations of the country, or other kinds of taxes which motivate behaviors designed to avoid tax rather than expand output. The developing countries need to pursue such efficiencies diligently, since they do not have the wealth that it costs to ignore good policy.

In this area as in numerous others, the elegantly simple and simply elegant wisdom of Henry George has left echoes in the halls of contemporary economics. He did not fall into the worn grooves of the ideologies that objective economists must try to avoid, but his perception of the implications of the actions and motives of economic agents informed his viewpoints and provided hints for the work of the present. The honesty of his exposition remains as an example for those who would wander into the world of policy; his caring for the truth and its demands on economic analysis remain aloft as a banner for the future.

Appendix: Henry George and the Reconstruction of Capitalism*

Robert V. Andelson

> It would require less than the fingers of the two hands to enumerate those who, from Plato down, rank with Henry George among the world's social philosophers ... [He is] certainly the greatest that this country has produced. No man ... has the right to regard himself as an educated man in social thought unless he has some first hand acquaintance with the theoretical contribution of this great American thinker.
>
> JOHN DEWEY

With the fall of the Iron Curtain, people all over the world seem to be searching for a "Middle Way." Except in North Korea and Cuba, doctrinaire Marxism has been repudiated virtually everywhere, even by the Left. Socialism has become passé. Its adherents are no longer riding the crest of the wave of the future. Even the most energetic apostles of federal meddling, John Kenneth Galbraith, for example, eschew the Socialist label.

Yet, on the other hand, the free market economists of the classical period would scarcely recognize Capitalism as we

---

* This appendix is reproduced with copyright permission from the Robert Schalkenbach Foundation, to whom I express deep appreciation. This wonderful essay appears on the website of the School of Cooperative Individualism: http://www.cooperativeindividualism.org/andelson-robert_henry-george-reconstruction-of-capitalism.html

know it in America today. Such luminaries of industry and finance as Lee Iacocca and Felix Rohatyn advocate a measure of government intervention that would have seemed entirely insupportable to Cobden or Ricardo. In the political field, the major candidates differ mainly on matters of degree. It is not so much a question of "Shall there be federal aid?" as of "How much federal aid shall there be?" or of "How shall it be administered?" As long ago as the late 1940s, "Mr. Conservative" himself, Senator Robert A. Taft, sponsored a bill for federal housing. Later, another Senate Republican leader, Bob Dole, was a major architect of the food stamp program, which is itself a dole, not just for the poor, but, above all, for agribusiness. A Republican president, Richard Nixon, instituted price controls, and cut the dollar loose from its last tenuous backing with the cynical quip, "We are all Keynesians now."

But what we are presented with, from Right to Left, is not a coordinated structure embodying the best elements from both sides, not even a well-thought-out attempt at syncretism, but rather a bewildering welter of jerry-built solutions, each one based on political and emotional considerations and lacking any functional relationship to a unified system of socio-economic truth – let alone any rootage in a grand scheme of teleology or ethics.

A little Socialism here, and a little Capitalism there; a concern for the public sector here, and a concession to the profit motive there; a sop to the "underprivileged" here, and a bow to incentive there—put them all together, and what have you got? Nothing but a great big rag-bag, a haphazard pastiche of odds and ends without any bones and without any guts!

Nevertheless, there is a Middle Way. There is a body of socio-economic truth which incorporates the best insights of both Capitalism and Socialism. Yet they are not insights that are artificially woven together to form a deliberate compromise. Instead, they arise naturally, with a kind of inner logic, from the profound ethical distinction which is the system's core. They arise remorselessly from an understanding of the meaning of the commandment: "Thou shalt not steal." This Middle Way is the philosophy associated with the name of Henry George.

I like to picture economic theory as a vast jigsaw puzzle distributed across two tables, one called Capitalism and the other, Socialism. But mingled with the genuine pieces of the puzzle are many false pieces, also distributed across both tables. Most of us are either perceptively limited to one table, or else we are unable to distinguish the genuine pieces from the false. But Henry George knew how to find the right pieces, and, therefore, he was able to put the puzzle together – at least in its general outlines. I don't claim that he was infallible, or that there isn't further work to be done. Yet if I find a little piece of puzzle missing here or there, it doesn't shake my confidence in the harmony of the overall pattern he discerned. It doesn't make me want to sweep the puzzle onto the floor and start all over again from scratch.

Henry George was born in 1839 in Philadelphia, and died in 1897 in New York City. It was in the San Francisco of the 1870s that he wrote his master-work, *Progress and Poverty*. For the greater part of his adult life he had been a working newspaperman, beginning as an apprentice typesetter and making his way up to the editor's desk. His was a peculiarly Californian saga. His philosophy was forged out of his observation of conditions in a burgeoning new state, where he was able to examine, as in a laboratory, the genesis and development of social and economic processes. *Progress and Poverty* has been translated into at least 27 languages.

Among books of nonfiction, its sale was for many decades exceeded only by the Bible. At Oxford University, in the English literature department, it is used as a model of the finest prose. The rest of Henry George's life was one great crusade for social justice, at the end of which he literally martyred himself by campaigning for public office against his doctors' urging. In the midst of the campaign he died, and was spontaneously accorded the greatest funeral that New York City had ever witnessed.

His genius has been glowingly acknowledged by such renowned figures as philosophers John Dewey and Mortimer J. Adler, presidents Woodrow Wilson and Dwight D. Eisenhower, scientists Alfred Russel Wallace and Albert Einstein, essayists John Ruskin and Albert Jay Nock, jurists Louis D. Brandeis and Samuel Seabury, columnists William F. Buckley and Michael Kinsley, and statesmen Winston Churchill and Sun Yat-sen. These names cover the entire political spectrum from Conservative to Liberal, yet all of them saw something of immense value in George's thought. I'll take time to quote from only one of these testimonials— the one by Dr. Sun Yat-sen, the founder and first president of the Republic of China. "I intend," he declared, "to devote my future to the welfare of the Chinese people. The teachings of Henry George will be the basis of our program of reform." I think we may safely say that had Dr. Sun lived to carry out his promise, the Chinese mainland would not today be Red. But Taiwan, where it has been carried out, by no means fully but to a considerable extent, has, as a result, witnessed a spectacular transformation from abysmal poverty to vibrant prosperity distributed so as to benefit all levels of the population.

I said that I'd quote from only one testimonial, and I'll keep my word. But I do consider it apposite to mention that Count Tolstoy, author of *War and Peace, Anna Karenina,* and of the explicitly Georgist novel, *Resurrection,* wrote a long letter to Tsar Nicholas 11 in January 1902, warning of mounting public disaffection, and pleading for reform along Georgist lines as the most immediate measure necessitated both by the demands of justice and the threat of socialist revolution. It was followed in May of the same year by a letter to another member of the imperial family, spelling out the specifics of George's proposal. May one not reasonably assume that, had Tolstoy's warning and plea been heeded, Russia would have been spared more than seven decades of Communist tyranny; its satellite and subject nations, their respective periods of Marxist domination; and the West, the burden of the Cold War? Or that, by disregarding that warning and that plea, Nicholas 11 forfeited the lives of hapless millions, including, ironically, his own and those of his cherished wife and children?

For a long time, it was the fashion among academic economists to ignore or patronize Henry George—whether for his lack of formal credentials, for his propensity to mingle moral arguments with economic ones, or for other perceived intellectual crimes even more monstrous. Today, this is becoming less and less the case, although, of course, there were honorable exceptions from the outset. But now we find economists of every stripe, including at least four Nobel laureates, united in agreement that George has much to say that is of vital contemporary importance. The list is far too long to read in its entirety, but it includes such names as Gary Becker, Kenneth Boulding, James Buchanan, Milton Friedman, Mason Gaffney, Lowell Harriss, Alfred Kahn, Arthur Laffer, Franco Modigliani, Warren Samuels, Robert Solow, James Tobin, and William Vickrey—the last of whom served recently as president of the American Economic Association.

In the preface to the fourth edition of *Progress and Poverty*, Henry George wrote: "What I have done in this book, if I have correctly solved the great problem I have sought to investigate, is to unite the truth perceived by the school of [Adam] Smith and Ricardo to the truth perceived by the schools of Proudhon and Lasalle; to show that laissez faire (in its full true meaning) opens the way to a realization of the noble dreams of socialism . . ." Let us return now to our illustration of the economic jigsaw puzzle, and take a look at the pieces which he selected from the two tables of Capitalism and Socialism.

We will begin with the Capitalist table. George considered himself a purifier of Capitalism, not its enemy. He built upon the foundations laid by the classical economists. The skeleton of his system is essentially Capitalist. In fact, Karl Marx referred to George's teaching as "Capitalism's last ditch." George believed in competition, in the free market, in the unrestricted operation of the laws of supply and demand. He distrusted government and despised bureaucracy. He was no egalitarian leveler; the only equality he sought was equal freedom of opportunity. Actually, what he intended was to make free enterprise truly free, by ridding it of the monopolistic hobbles which prevent its effective operation.

In his book, *The Condition of Labor,* George said: "We differ from the Socialists in our diagnosis of the evil, and we differ from them in remedies. We have no fear of capital, regarding it as the natural handmaiden of labor; we look on interest in itself as natural and just; we would set no limit to accumulation, nor impose on the rich any burden that is not equally placed on the poor; we see no evil in competition, but deem unrestricted competition to be as necessary to the health of the industrial and social organism as the free circulation of the blood is to the bodily organism— to be the agency whereby the fullest cooperation is to be secured."

Why did George take so many pieces from the Capitalist table? Because, I think, they are all corollaries of one big piece, namely, the moral justification for private property. You see, George, who was a devout though non-sectarian Christian, had a stout belief in the God-given dignity of the individual. This dignity, he held, demands that we recognize that the individual possesses an absolute and inalienable right to himself, which is forfeited only when he refuses to accord the same right to others. The right to one's self implies the right to one's labor, which is an extension of one's self, and therefore to the product of one's labor – to use it, to enjoy it, to give it away, to destroy it, to bequeath it, or even (if one so desires) to bury it in the ground.

Now, taxation as ordinarily understood, especially when based upon the "ability to pay" principle, is a denial of this right. It is a denial of it because it represents a tribute levied on the product of an individual's labor. It is a denial of it because it rests upon the assumption that the community at large has a right to assess individuals disproportionately to the benefits which they receive from the community at large. And so George rejects as collectivistic many institutions that most present-day defenders of free enterprise would never dream of questioning – income taxes, tariffs, sales taxes, corporate taxes, personal property taxes, etc. This makes him in one sense an arch-Conservative, yet prominent Socialists like Walter Rauschenbusch and George Bernard Shaw have testified that it was Henry George who first kindled their concern for social justice. To understand the reason for this, we must direct our attention to the other table, the table labeled "Socialism."

In fitting together the economic jigsaw puzzle, George took only two pieces from the Socialist table. But what large and what strategic pieces they were! The first of these was his insistence that all persons come into the world with an equal right of access to the goods of nature. The second was his contention that the community has a right to take that which the community produces.

Actually, these pieces had landed on the Socialist table only by default. They had originally been part of the theory of Capitalism, as outlined by John Locke, the Physiocrats, and Adam Smith. But Capitalism in practice ignored them, and so became a distorted caricature. George's notion was to rescue these lost elements, and restore balance and proportion to the Capitalist table.

Now, if private property derives its moral justification from the right of a human being to the fruits of his or her own efforts, clearly the land and the other goods of nature do not belong in the category of private property because no human efforts created them. And the value that attaches to them is not the result of anything their title-holder does to them; it is the result of the presence and activity of the community around them. Someone can build a skyscraper in the desert and the ground upon which it stands will not be worth a penny more because of it, yet a city lot with nothing on it may be worth a fortune simply because of the number of people who pass by it daily.

Why, asked Henry George in effect, should private individuals be allowed to fatten upon the unearned increment of land—upon the rise in value which the community creates because of population increase and the growth of public services? Why should certain people be allowed to levy tribute upon others who desire access to their common heritage? But, you might object, the present owner may have paid hard-earned money for his land. Has he not, therefore, a vested right? To this, George would have answered: If one unwittingly buys stolen goods, the rectitude of one's intentions establishes no right against the legitimate owner of those goods.

Henry George was not the first thinker to comprehend the difference between land and other kinds of property. John Locke said that "God gave the world in common to all mankind. . . . When the 'sacredness' of property is talked of, it should be remembered that any such sacredness does not belong in the same degree to landed property." William Blackstone wrote: "The earth, and all things therein, are the general property of all man-kind, from the immediate gift of the Creator." Thomas Paine stated that "men did not make the earth . . . It is the value of the improvements only, and not the earth itself, that is individual property." According to Thomas Jefferson, "The earth is given as a common stock for men to labor and live on."

John Stuart Mill wrote: "The increase in the value of land, arising as it does from the efforts of an entire community, should belong to the community and not to the individual who might hold title." Abraham Lincoln said: "The land, the earth God gave to man for his home, sustenance, and support, should never be the possession of any man, corporation, society, or unfriendly government, any more than the air or water, if as much." In the words of Herbert Spencer, "equity does not permit property in land...The world is God's bequest to mankind. All men are joint heirs to it."

But it was Henry George who emphasized this distinction and placed it at the very center of his system. At present we have the ironic spectacle of the community penalizing the individual for his industry and initiative, and taking away from him a share of that which he produces, while at the same time lavishing upon the nonproducer undeserved windfalls which it—the community—produces. Henry George built his whole program around the principle: Let the individual keep all of that which he or she produces, and let the community keep all of that which it produces.

Land monopoly is the great monkey-wrench which is caught in the works of the free enterprise system, and which prevents the proper meshing of its gears; it is the hidden cancer that is eating out the heart of Capitalism. Early in this century, a great statesman described its virulent effects in the following words:

> While the land is what is called "ripening" for the unearned increment of its owner, the merchant going to his office and the artisan going to his work must detour or pay a fare to avoid it. The people lose their chance of using the land, the city and state lose the taxes which would have accrued if the natural development had taken place, and all the while the land monopolist has only to sit still and watch complacently his property multiplying in value, sometimes many fold, without either effort or contribution on his part.

> This evil process strikes at every form of industrial activity. The municipality, wishing for broader streets, better houses, more

healthy, decent, scientifically planned towns, is made to pay more to get them in proportion as it has exerted itself to make past improvements. The more it has improved the town, the more it will have to pay for any land it may now wish to acquire for further improvements.

The manufacturer proposing to start a new industry, proposing to erect a great factory offering employment to thousands of hands, is made to pay such a price for his land that the purchase price hangs around the neck of his whole business, hampering his competitive power in every market, clogging him far more than any foreign tariff in his export competition, and the land price strikes down through the profits of the manufacturer on to the wages of the workman.

No matter where you look or what examples you select, you will see that every form of enterprise, every step in material progress, is only undertaken after the land monopolist has skimmed the cream off for himself, and everywhere today the man or the public body that wishes to put land to its highest use is forced to pay a preliminary fine in land values to the man who is putting it to an inferior use, and in some cases to no use at all. All comes back to the land value, and its owner is able to levy toll upon all other forms of wealth and every form of industry.

Those were the words of Winston Churchill. And if you will examine the history of the major American depressions, you will find that virtually every one of them was preceded by a period of intense land speculation which had an inflationary effect upon the whole economy. In 1836, in 1857, in 1873, in 1893, and in 1929 – in every instance, the big crash was precipitated by the bursting of the land bubble.

The purely economic ramifications of land monopoly are so vast as to be staggering. Land monopoly does not affect rents alone. It affects wages, prices, production, the cost of government, and the distribution of purchasing power. It is the major cause of slums and blighted areas. It is the greatest single breeder of revolution around the world.

Had it not been for land monopoly, the Bolsheviks could never have gained power in Russia. Mao Tse-tung and his so-called "agrarian reformers" (and I use that term advisedly) could never have wrested control of China. Fidel Castro would never have arisen in Cuba. Because of land monopoly, El Salvador has endured decades of murderous civil war. Because of land monopoly, the Amazon rain forest is being rapidly destroyed to make room for settlers who have been denied a foothold elsewhere except on terms that offer little better than starvation. These are just a few obvious examples, taken almost at random. Because of land monopoly, Latin America and the Middle East are veritable tinder boxes, ready to explode at any moment. We in the U.S. may not yet have reached that state, but we're moving in that direction. How much longer can we go on propping up a rotten structure by borrowing against the future?

Well, exactly how did Henry George propose to deal with the problem of land monopoly? Did he advocate that privately held land should be expropriated and divided up? Quite the contrary. That remedy is as ultimately ineffective as it is ancient. There is more truth than fiction in the aphorism that the French Revolution delivered the peasants from the aristocrats only to hand them over to the usurers, and what was true of the peasants was equally true of the soil they tilled. Thus has it ever been with programs of expropriation and redistribution.

Under Henry George's system, private land titles would not be disturbed one iota. No one would be expropriated. Instead, the community would simply take something approaching the total annual economic rent of land for public purposes. This amount would be determined by the value of each site on the free market, not by any arbitrary governmental fiat. In other words, the privilege of monopolizing a site is a benefit received from society and for which society should be fully compensated; and so, under the Georgist system, the person who wished to monopolize a site would pay a rent for it to the community, approaching 100 percent of its annual rental value, exclusive of improvements.

Let me emphasize that last phrase, "exclusive of improvements." The apartment house owner would pay the full value of his lot, and nothing on his building; the factory owner would pay the full value of his site, and nothing on his factory; the farmer would pay the full value of his ground, and nothing on his structures or his crop, his livestock or his machinery; the homeowner would pay the full value of his lot, and nothing on his house. If the land had no market value, the owner would pay nothing; if it had a value, he would pay regardless of whether he were using it or deriving income from it.

This would, of course, eliminate all speculative profit in landholding, squeeze the "speculative water" out of land prices, and in effect bring back the frontier by making cheap land readily available to everyone—at least initially. The result would be to raise the margin of production, increase real wages, and stimulate building and productivity. Eventually, the flourishing economy would cause use value to exceed the former speculative value, but instead of being engrossed by those who make no contribution to the economy, land rent would flow into the public coffers in place of taxes levied upon labor and capital. The land-value charge is really what Walt Wryneck so aptly calls "a super user's fee." For the privilege of exclusive access to and disposition of a site and its natural resources, the owner pays an indemnity to those who are thereby dispossessed—an indemnity reflecting precisely the market value of his privilege, collected through the tax mechanism and relieving them of the burden of payment for public services. What could be more fair?

Actually, I daresay that each one of you, probably without realizing it, frequently pays something that partakes of the principle of such a "super user's fee" whether you own land or not. Every time you put money in a parking meter, you are purchasing a temporary monopoly of the parking space.

Don't ever complain about having to put money in a public parking meter; it's a bargain for you. You're getting a free gift from the community – the difference between what you pay and what a commercial parking lot in the vicinity would charge!

I have spoken of land monopoly as a cancer, and so it is. Yet land often cannot be used efficiently unless monopolized. The Georgist remedy does not provide for the excision of land monopoly but rather for its transformation from malignant to benign. For the monopoly of land can be fair and even salutary if the monopolizer pays into the public treasury a sum that reflects substantially the market value of his privilege.

Perhaps this would be a good place to interject that when economists speak of "land," they are talking about nature. The term embraces not only space on the earth's surface but also natural resources—oil in the ground, virgin timber, wildlife, the oceans and other natural bodies of water, the airwaves, airspace, etc. To capture for the public the value of these natural goods, land-value charges may in some cases need to be supplanted by or combined with other methods such as severance taxes and auctioning of leases. But the principle is the same.

If time were not limited, I could talk at length about specific advantages of the Georgist system. I could go into the "canons of taxation," and show how it fulfills better than any other method these ideal criteria whereby economists measure the effectiveness of a system of public revenue. I could give concrete illustrations of how it is working right now in Denmark, in Australia, in New Zealand, in Taiwan, and even in some areas in the U.S.

This is not the idle pipe-dream of an armchair visionary. It has been tested by experience. Let me just cite the Hutchinson Report, a survey comparing the various Australian states in terms of the degree to which they use the Henry George approach. It found that wages, purchasing power, growth of industry, volume of retail sales, land under cultivation, value of improvements, and population gain through immigration from other states were in every case greater in direct ratio to the proportion of revenues derived from the public collection of ground rent. To me, this is the most conclusive argument anyone could ask for!

Of course, Henry George's proposal has nowhere been fully implemented. Even where it has been implemented substantially, its beneficial impact has invariably been blunted by countervailing policies, oftentimes at other levels of government. It is not a panacea. To be completely effective, it would need to be supplemented by other reforms, such as measures to assure a stable currency. But of it this much can be said: All other systems have been found wanting. This alone has worked whenever and wherever it has been tried to the extent that it has been tried. I submit that it is now deserving of actualization on a broader and more thoroughgoing scale.

Nobody, to my knowledge, advocates that it be instituted whole-hog overnight. But it could be phased in in easy stages so as to obviate the risk of shock and dislocation. And it is my considered opinion that, by the time the system were in full effect, the revenues produced by collecting land values alone would suffice to meet all legitimate public needs. This may not have been true during the Cold War, with its staggering burden of nuclear defense. But with that burden lifted, and with the need for welfare of all kinds evaporated because of the full employment and other social benefits that the system would naturally engender, and for other reasons, which time precludes my specifying here, I really think that we could dispense with taxes on incomes, improvements, sales, imports, and all the rest. If I am unduly optimistic in this belief, and the public appropriation of land-values were insufficient, this would be no argument against using it as far as it could go.

There are two things which a government can never do and still be just: The first of these is to take for public purposes what rightfully belongs to private individuals or corporations. The second is to give to private individuals or corporations what rightfully belongs to the public. All wealth that is privately produced rightfully belongs to private individuals or corporations, and for the government to appropriate it is unjust. But land rent is publicly produced, and for the government to give it to private individuals or corporations is equally unjust. He who thinks himself prepared to justify in principle the private monopolization of land rent, must also be prepared to justify in principle the jobbery of the Tweed Ring and the looting of Teapot Dome—not to mention the escapades of Michael Milken, Ivan Boesky, and Charles Keating.

In closing, I will summarize with a quotation from the late Dr. Viggo Starke, for many years a member of the Danish cabinet: "What I produce is mine. All mine! What you produce is yours. All yours! But that which none of us produced, but which we all lend value to together, belongs by right to all of us in common." This, in a nutshell, is the philosophy of Henry George.

The above appendix is reproduced from
http://www.cooperativeindividualism.org/andelson-robert_
henry-george-reconstruction-of-capitalism.html

Notes

Chapter 1

1. Henry George, *A Perplexed Philosopher, Being an Examination of Mr. Herbert Spencer's Various Utterances on the Land Question, with Some Incidental Reference to His Synthetic Philosophy.* The Legacy and Works of Henry George in CD Format, 2001 (Boston, MA: Lincoln Institute of Land Policy, 1892), p. 1.
2. Ibid.
3. See Robert M. Solow, "How to Treat Intellectual Ancestors," in H. James Brown, ed., *Land Use and Taxation* (Cambridge, MA: Lincoln Institute of Land Policy, 1997), p. 14.
4. Joseph Schumpeter, *The History of Economic Analysis* (Oxford: Oxford University Press, 1954), pp. 864, 865.
5. Ibid.
6. Ibid.
7. Ibid.
8. Henry George, *The Science of Political Economy, A Reconstruction of Its Principles in Clear and Systematic Form.* The Legacy and Works of Henry George in CD Format, 2001 (Boston, MA: Lincoln Institute of Land Policy, 1898), p. 97. This work was published posthumously and is based on a not fully completed manuscript.
9. Ibid., pp. 97, 98.
10. Ibid., p. 102.
11. Ibid.
12. Ibid., pp. 29, 30.
13. Ibid., p. 28.
14. Ibid.

15. George, *Science of Political Economy*, p. 165. George attributes this quote of 1856 to Professor J. E. Cairnes, to lectures delivered at Dublin University to the Whately Foundation. The lectures were later reprinted under the title "The Character and Logical Method of Political Economy."
16. Ibid., p. 165.
17. Henry George, *Progress and Poverty, An Inquiry into the Cause of Industrial Depressions and of Increase of Want with Increase of Wealth. The Remedy,* San Francisco. The Legacy and Works of Henry George in CD Format, 2001 (Boston, MA: Lincoln Institute of Land Policy, 1879), footnote, p. 100.
18. See Alfred Marshall, "On Rent," *Economic Journal,* Vol. 3, No. 9, Mar. 1893, p. 82.
19. Marshall, op. cit.
20. Ibid.
21. Ibid.
22. Ibid., p. 117.
23. Ibid., p. 134.
24. Ibid., p. 167.
25. Ibid.
26. Ibid., p. 151.
27. Ibid., pp. 268, 269.
28. Ibid., p. 159.
29. Ibid., p. 160.
30. Ibid., p. 137.
31. Ibid., p. 139.
32. Ibid., p. 310.
33. See ibid., p. 302.
34. Ibid., p. 304.
35. Ibid., p. 121.
36. Ibid., p. 126.
37. Ibid., p. 128.
38. Ibid.
39. Ibid., p. 185.
40. See Note 4.
41. George, *Science of Political Economy,* p. 197.
42. Ibid.
43. Ibid., p. 220.
44. Ibid., p. 226.

45. George cites Walker's *Political Economy*, 3rd Edition (New York: Henry Holt, 1888), which says "Wealth comprises all articles of value and nothing else." Section 7.
46. George, *Science of Political Economy*, pp. 282–83. Interestingly, in another passage, George refers to the seller of newspapers as being in production, since the newspaper represents wealth.
47. Ibid., pp. 236–37.
48. Ibid., p. 273.
49. Ibid., pp. 340, 341.
50. Ibid., p. 342.
51. Ibid., p. 349.
52. Ibid.

Chapter 2

1. The biographical source on Henry George serving as the foundation for this chapter is the highly reputed and authoritative biography written by George's son, Henry George Jr. There are numerous sources with material on his life, but this one tells the complete and appropriately positive story of Henry George. For the less ambitious reader, many biographical treatments are available. An excellent short one is Mason Gaffney (1997), and one also finds good, basic information at the Wikipedia site on Henry George.
2. Joseph Schumpeter (1954) characterized this kind of originality as *subjective originality*. Schumpeter noted that some important analyses (e.g., the marginal analysis of economics developed at about the same time, independently, by William Stanley Jevons in England, Leon Walras in France, and Carl Menger in Austria) are produced with subjective originality even though they may have already been developed elsewhere by some other individual achieving *objective originality*.

Chapter 3

1. George never made it across the bridge to the neoclassical world. Mark Blaug writes of *Progress and Poverty* that it was a "wonderful example of old-style classical economics," but

"thirty years out of date the day it was published." See Mark Blaug, *Economic Theory in Retrospect,* 3rd Edition (London: Cambridge University Press, 1978), p. 88.

2. Henry George, *Progress and Poverty: An Inquiry into the Cause of Industrial Depressions and of Increase of Want with Increase of Wealth . . . The Remedy* (San Francisco, D. Appleton & Company). The version cited here was republished on CD, 2001 (Boston, MA: Lincoln Institute of Land Policy, 1879), p. 163.

3. Ibid., p. 36.

4. Ibid., p. 38.

5. Ibid., pp. 71, 72.

6. This point is discussed in Robert F. Hebert, "Marshall: A Professional Economist Guards the Purity of His Discipline – Part II: Nineteenth-century British and Continental Critics," *The American Journal of Economics and Sociology,* Nov., 2003.

7. Paul A. Samuelson, "The Classical Fallacy," *Journal of Economic Literature,* Vol. 32, No. 2, Jun., 1994, pp. 620–39.

8. Ibid.

9. All of these statements come from Alfred Marshall, 1920. *Principles of Economics,* 9th Edition, p. 823.

10. Ibid., p. 629.

11. Ibid.

12. I presented an outline of this approach to George's distribution theory earlier at a conference. See Phillip J. Bryson, "Henry George: The Theory of Distribution in Progress and Poverty," *Review of Business Research,* Vol. 7, No. 4, 2007, pp. 20–24.

13. George, *Progress and Poverty,* p. 186.

14. Ibid., pp. 238, 239.

15. Ibid., p. 223.

16. Ibid., p. 224.

17. Ibid., p. 255.

18. Hebert, op. cit.

19. Marshall, *Principles of Economics,* p. 505.

20. See Blaug, op. cit., pp. 86, 87.

21. See ibid., p. 86 where Blaug concludes that "In long-run stationary equilibrium, the total product is resolvable into wages and interest as payments to labor and capital—there is

no third factor of production—and the theory of differential rent is interesting only because it marks the first appearance of the marginal principle in economic theory."

22. Ibid., p. 87.

23. Marshall, *Principles of Economics,* pp. 514, 515.

24. This is a basic point in the analysis of Hebert, op. cit. See also Marshall's "On Rent," *Economic Journal,* Vol. 3, No. 9, Mar., 1893, pp. 74–90, which deals quite clearly with these issues. Marshall observed that it was difficult for people steeped in Ricardian doctrines from early in the 1800s to accept a new analysis and realize that Ricardo's work had been freed from "the encumbrance of dead dogmas" (p. 74). He reviewed the notion of producer's surplus as the excess of the gross receipts a producer gets for any of his commodities over their prime cost. He wrote that, generally speaking, the prices and quantities firms choose are determined by the relations of demand and supply. The market price must cover the cost of production of that quantity "raised at the greatest disadvantage" (p. 78), and the remainder of the quantity produced yields a surplus.

25. Marshall, *Principles of Economics,* pp. 513, 514. According to Marshall's own summary,

> in a comprehensive, if difficult, statement:—Every agent of production, land, machinery, skilled labour, unskilled labour, etc., tends to be applied in production as far as it profitably can be. If employers, and other business men, think that they can get a better result by using a little more of any one agent they will do so. They estimate the net product (that is the net increase of the money value of their total output after allowing for incidental expenses) that will be got by a little more outlay in this direction, or a little more outlay in that; and if they can gain by shifting a little of their outlay from one direction to another, they will do so.
>
> (See p. 521)

26. Ibid., pp. 357ff.

27. Good sources for an informal, online study of the uses of mathematics in economics are available and can be located with a Google search or two.
28. Ibid., pp. 846, 847.
29. See Blaug, op. cit., pp.460-63.
30. Joan Robinson, *Accumulation of Capital* (London: Palgrave Macmillan, 1956), pp. 109–10.
31. See Luigi L. Pasinetti and Roberto Scazzieri, "Capital Theory: Paradoxes," in John Eatwell, Murray Milgate, and Peter Newman, eds., *The New Palgrave: A Dictionary of Economics, Vol. I.* (Houndmills: Palgrave Macmillan, 1987), pp. 363–68.
32. See Piero Sraffa, *Production of Commodities by Means of Commodities* (Cambridge: Cambridge University Press, 1960).
33. Ibid., p. 367.
34. David C. Lincoln has reminded me that we don't need all the refinements and exploration of high theory to appreciate some basic principles that would occur, say, to a thoughtful businessman. His view of George is that he was, like most economists, interested in overcoming the injustice of monopoly. The monopolists of his day were mostly landholders and George simply proposed a tax on their monopoly earnings.
35. Blaug, op. cit., p. 87.
36. George, *Progress and Poverty,* p. 338.
37. See Henry George, Jr., *The Life of Henry George* (Honolulu, Hawaii: University Press of the Pacific, 2004, reprinted from the 1900 edition).
38. Hebert, op. cit., p. 39.
39. Ibid., p. 40.
40. Marshall, "On Rent," p. 78.
41. Ibid.
42. Ibid.
43. This section owes much to the excellent article by John J. Whitaker, "Enemies or Allies? Henry George and Francis Amasa Walker One Century Later," *Journal of Economic Literature,* Vol. XXXV, No. 4, Dec., 1997, pp. 1891–915.
44. Ibid., p. 1893.
45. Ibid., p.1895.

46. Ibid., p. 232.
47. Marshall, too, observed that empirical data failed to support George's assumption that rents had been rising while wages and interest declined. See more on this point in Hebert, op. cit.
48. Whitaker, op.cit., p. 1905.
49. Henry George's "Principles and Plan Outlined," Preface to 4th edition. *Progress and Poverty An Inquiry into the Cause of Industrial Depressions and of Increase of Want with Increase of Wealth . . . The Remedy* (San Fransisco, 1879). Taken from the introduction.
50. George, *Progress and Poverty*, pp. 238, 239.
51. Ibid., p. 223.
52. Ibid., p. 224.
53. Ibid., pp. 357ff.
54. Ibid., pp. 846, 847.

Chapter 4

1. Henry George, *Protection or Free Trade: An Examination of the Tariff Question, with Especial Regard to the Interests of Labor* (Boston, MA: Lincoln Institute of Land Policy, republished from original appearance in 1886), p. 7.
2. Ibid., p. 12.
3. Ibid., p. 18.
4. Ibid.
5. Ibid., p. 25.
6. Ibid., p. 32.
7. George's conclusion is implicit in his framing of the question as to whether specialization and trade are not appropriate at the level of the family, region, or nation. Of this he writes:

> It seems to me impossible to consider the necessarily universal character of the protective theory without feeling it to be repugnant to moral perceptions and inconsistent with the simplicity and harmony which we everywhere discover in natural law. What should we think of human laws framed for the government

of a country which should compel each family to keep constantly on their guard against every other family, to expend a large part of their time and labor in preventing exchanges with their neighbors, and to seek their own prosperity by opposing the natural efforts of other families to become prosperous? Yet the protective theory implies that laws such as these have been imposed by the Creator upon the families of men who tenant this earth. It implies that by virtue of social laws, as immutable as the physical laws, each nation must stand jealously on guard against every other nation and erect artificial obstacles to national intercourse.

(See ibid., p. 33)

8. The evidence shows that ocean freight rates have actually increased in the postwar period, but air freight rates have declined rather rapidly. The cost of overland transport has actually declined as compared with that of ocean transport. All the transportation modes have experienced declining freight costs associated with increased distance. See David Hummels, *Have International Transportation Costs Declined?* (University of Chicago, Jul., 1999). Available online at: http://www.aerohabitat.eu/uploads/media/11-01-2006_-_D_Hummels__Transportation_cost_declines.pdf

9. I remember taking a quasi-antediluvian undergraduate international economics course that explicitly built transportation costs into the basic analysis. As the years went by and I began teaching the course, it struck me how convenient it was that such costs became basically insignificant, at least for a first pass at the benefits of international specialization and trade. Taking transportation costs into account in modeling for policy purposes does not enable improved performance in predicting evolving trade patterns or in explaining changes in the complex, overall trade patterns. Mark Gehlhar explains that the transportation variable is important in policy simulation models. See his *Incorporating Transportation Costs into International Trade Models: Theory and Application,* Economic Research Service, USDA. This article is no longer available online.

10. See ibid.
11. With total cost (or CP) $=$ PC $+$ TC $+$ TrC $+$ STrC, for simplification let transport, transactions, and tariff costs all be constant. For a given distance, prevailing tariff rates, et cetera, the assumption need not be unrealistic. Let production cost, $PC = a + bQ + CQ^2 + dQ^3$, so that $MC = b + 2CQ + 3dQ^2$. With a simple demand function, $MPreg = \alpha - \beta Q$, the total revenue function would be $MPreg (Q) = \alpha Q - \beta Q^2$, so that $MC = \alpha - 2\beta Q$. The net revenue maximizing expression would be $b + 2CQ + 3dQ^2 = \alpha - 2\beta Q$. The exporting firm would solve for Q, the amount of the product to be sold at MPreg, the regional market price in the targeted area. Note that so long as all the transactions-type costs are constant, the optimal level of exports to the targeted country is determined by the regional market price and the characteristics of the production costs. The optimal sales level will be indicated at the output where the total cost curve is at the maximum possible distance above the total revenue curve. Although the slopes of the two curves are determined as mentioned, the level of the total PC curve shifts up as fixed costs are greater. This will simply reduce the level of net revenues accruing to the optimal sales level.
12. See George, op. cit., p. 34.
13. Ibid.
14. Ibid., p. 34.
15. Ibid., p. 47.
16. Ibid., p. 49.
17. Ibid., p. 51
18. Ibid.
19. Ibid., p. 52.
20. Ibid., pp. 53, 54.
21. Ibid., p. 68.
22. For a modern treatment of this issue and for a number of related insights, see Edward Gresser, "Toughest on the Poor: America's Flawed Tariff System," *Foreign Affairs,* Nov./Dec., 2002.
23. See George, op. cit., p. 69.
24. Ibid., p. 73.

25. Ibid., p. 75.
26. Ibid., p. 84.
27. See ibid., p. 131. It should be pointed out that a widely read refutation of applying tariffs as a retaliatory measure was debunked (again, doubtless) by Milton Friedman nearly 50 years ago in his *Capitalism and Freedom* (Chicago, IL: University of Chicago Press, 1962).
28. See ibid., p. 79. For a contemporary source, see Harry G. Johnson, "Optimum Tariffs and Retaliation," *Review of Economic Studies,* Vol. 21, No. 2, 1954, pp. 142–53. The notion seems to have developed from Charles F. Bickerdike, "The Theory of Incipient Taxes," *Economic Journal,* Vol. 16, Dec., 1906, pp. 529–35.
29. Ibid., p. 80. George added in a most entertaining manner: "And it is well for mankind that this is so. If it were possible for the government of one country, by any system of taxation, to compel the people of other countries to pay its expenses, the world would soon be taxed into barbarism."
30. See Steven Suranavic's convenient exposition, "The Stolper-Samuelson Theorem: Mathematical Derivation," Available online at: http://internationalecon.com/v1.0/ch115/115c020.html, accessed on March 30, 2011.
31. Thomas L. Martin, "Protection or Free Trade: An Analysis of the Ideas of Henry George on International Commerce and Wages," *The American Journal of Economics and Sociology,* Vol. 60, No. 5, Nov., 2001, pp. 119–36.
32. This reasoning is seconded by Lawrence S. Moss, "Why the Preaching Must Never Stop: Henry George's and Paul Krugman's Respective Contributions to the Free Trade Debate," *The American Journal of Economics and Sociology,* Vol. 60, No. 5, Nov., 2001, pp 137-64. Moss writes: "when we read George we learn the opposite: the gains from free trade at least in the short run will benefit the laborers and not the landowners. For a while, free trade brings higher wages and relatively lower rents."

> Could George be claiming that in America it is land and not labor that has become scarcer? I think he was maintaining exactly this point. George insisted that,

under the social conditions of his time, the creation of exclusive property rights in land and the sport of trying to make speculative profits made land scarcer and that this is the source of the great social injustice that harms labor in the long run.

33. See Fred Harrison, "Longe and Wrightson: Conservative Critics of George's Wage Theory," *The American Journal of Economics and Sociology,* Vol. 62, No. 5, Nov., 2003, pp. 83–115. Harrison competently discusses George's wages theory at length. For the present point, see his page 84.

34. See ibid., pp. 85–90. Harrison writes:

> Wage theory today still relies on the concept of marginal productivity, but there has been a shift in the perspective. George approached the problem from the supply side: how much a free labourer who had access to marginal land would require in wages before giving up his self-employed status. Today, theorists focus on the demand side: how many workers would be hired by employers at ruling wage rates. But the basic equation remains as George defined it: equilibrium is that point where the marginal *physical* product of labour = marginal revenue to the firm = the marginal wage.

35. See George, op. cit., p. 175.

36. The quoted phrases are from ibid., p. 176. In this passage, George excoriated such industries:

> The cry of "protection for American labor" comes most vociferously from newspapers that lie under the ban of the printers' unions; from coal and iron lords who, importing "pauper labor" by wholesale, have bitterly fought every effort of their men to claim anything like decent wages; and from factory owners who claim the right to dictate the votes of men. The whole spirit of protection is against the rights of labor.

37. Ibid., p. 178.

38. Ibid.
39. Ibid., p. 179.
40. Ibid., p. 180.
41. Ibid., pp. 184, 185.
42. Ibid., p. 226.
43. Ibid., p. 227.
44. Ibid., p. 235.
45. Ibid., p. 237.
46. Ibid., p. 86.
47. George's colorful description of the politics of protection can be reviewed in ibid., pp. 87–89.
48. Ibid.
49. Ibid., pp. 89, 90
50. Ibid., p. 95.
51. Ibid., p. 18.
52. Ibid., p. 157.
53. George writes that "even where we import largely from such countries as Brazil, which have almost no manufactures of their own, we cannot send them in return the manufactured goods they want, but to pay for what we buy of them must send our raw materials to Europe." (See ibid., p. 158). The question of the structure of colonial imports and exports is an interesting one, but there is little space for it here. The interested reader might consult a healthy literature, including Douglas A. Irwin, *Antebellum Tariff Politics: Coalition Formation and Shifting Regional Interests,* NBER Working Paper No. W12161, 2006a. This paper focuses on an earlier period than that in which George wrote, although George, too, was interested in the whole span of U.S. history, including the colonial period. Irwin makes the point that import tariffs have been on a sustained downward path in only two instances in U.S. history, that is, from the early 1830s until the Civil War and from the mid-1930s to the present. Here, we are more interested in George's perceptions and theories than in the rather commendable accuracy of his casual observation, which correctly perceived the strength of the protectionist forces of his day. See also by Irwin, *Tariff Incidence in America's Gilded Age,* NBER Working Paper No. W12162, Apr., 2006b. Available online at SSRN:

http://ssrn.com/abstract=896470, accessed on March 30, 2011.
54. Ibid., p. 159.
55. See ibid., p. 162, where George concludes that

> there is not a first-class ocean carrier under the American flag, and but for the fact that foreign vessels are absolutely prohibited from carrying between American ports, shipbuilding, in which we once led the world, would now be with us a lost art. As it is, we have utterly lost our place.

56. Ibid., pp. 166, 167.
57. Ibid., p. 194.
58. For his strong statement on this, see ibid., p. 197.
59. George did observe the following:

> It is true that statistics may be arrayed in such way as to prove to the satisfaction of those who wish to believe it, that the condition of the working-classes is steadily improving. But that this is not the fact working-men well know. It is true that the average consumption has increased, and that the cheapening of commodities has brought into common use things that were once considered luxuries. It is also true that in many trades wages have been somewhat raised and hours reduced by combinations among workmen. But although the prizes that are to be gained in the lottery of life—or, if any one prefers so to call them, the prizes that are to be gained by superior skill, energy and foresight—are constantly becoming greater and more glittering, the blanks grow more numerous.
>
> (See ibid., p. 201)

60. See ibid., pp. 217–18.

Chapter 5

1. Henry George, *Our Land and Land Policy: Speeches, Lectures, and Miscellaneous Writings* (Boston, MA: Lincoln Institute

of Land Policy, Republished from the original appearance in New York: Doubleday and McClure Company, 1902), p. 30.

2. Ibid., p. 70.
3. Ibid.
4. Ibid., p. 71.
5. Directly quoted phrases are from ibid., p. 104.
6. Ibid., p. 137.
7. This oration is included in the same publication by the Lincoln Institute as *Our Land and Land Policy.*
8. Ibid., p. 150.
9. Ibid., p. 138.
10. Ibid., p. 157.
11. Ibid., p. 158.
12. Ibid., p. 163.
13. Ibid., p. 167.
14. Ibid., pp. 190, 191.
15. Henry George, *Social Problems* (Boston, MA: Lincoln Institute of Land Policy, Republished from the original appearance in New York: Doubleday and McClure Company, 1883), p. 12.
16. Ibid.
17. Ibid., p. 13.
18. Ibid. It is possible that this passage was neither a prophecy nor a description of the U.S. financial reform legislation of 2010.
19. Ibid., pp. 46, 47.
20. Ibid., p. 48.
21. Ibid., pp. 50, 51. Perhaps George was not the only one to be motivated to write this passage by the phenomenon of ripened public sector unions in the United States at the advent of this new century.
22. Ibid., p. 53.
23. Ibid.
24. Ibid., p. 74.
25. Ibid., p. 77.
26. Ibid., pp. 160–61.
27. Ibid., p. 112.
28. Ibid., p. 138.

29. This publication was later renamed *The Land Question*.
30. Juergen G. Backhaus, 1997. *Land Value Taxation in Germany: Theoretical and Historical Issues*. Essay prepared for a Compendium on Land Value Taxation Around the World to be published on the occasion of the 100th anniversary of the death of Henry George. Available online at: http://landtax. co.il., accessed on Aug. 26, 1997., p. 22.
31. Foldvary (1999, p. 185) presents this succinctly by considering two cornfields of equal area. Assuming the same quality and amount of labor and capital are applied to both, one will produce ten bushels per season, the other eight. If the farmer can get the eight-bushel land for free, he would pay two bushels to use the ten-bushel land, so returns to labor after rent are the same. Competition equalizes the returns after rent, with the extra product from the superior land being land rent. Thus, the market rent in this case is twenty bushels. Rent is due simply to the differential between the productivity of the two land parcels.

    As this small farming community grows and demand for agricultural output increases commensurately, the "margin of production" moves to the eight bushel land. This will cause wages to decline to eight. Rent would now be one on nine bushel land and two on ten bushel land. With increasing population the margin moves to less productive lands, wages decrease while rent keeps rising. When the margin is at very unproductive levels, wages are likewise at poverty or subsistence levels and the increment of production accrues to the landowners as rent. Thus we have George's poverty in the midst of progress.
32. The points made here regarding the benefits and problems associated with the property tax are made very effectively by Jorge Martinez-Vazquez and Mark Rider, "The Assignment of the Property Tax: Should Developing Countries Follow the Conventional Wisdom?" "What Role for Property Taxes?" Conference: Andrew Young School of Policy Studies, International Studies Program, Georgia State University and The Lincoln Institute of Land Policy, Apr. 27-29, 2008. Available online at: http://aysps.gsu.edu, accessed on Oct. 29, 2010.

Chapter 6

1. I first encountered Henry George as a young boy, long before I was ready to consider making economics my profession, when my parents purchased a set of "classical" books devoted to literature, science, history, and philosophy. These books were the "greatest produced by American writers." Henry George's *magnum opus* was the only book on economics in the set. I confess that it took several decades before I actually got around to reading it.

2. George's work has been put into an appropriate, positive perspective by Andelson (2004). Since Henry George's theories have proved capable of surviving a century of criticism, Andelson suggests, among social scientists and philosophers he was "not a mortal theorist but a veritable god." Although there is among some a false understanding of Georgism, it is not a cult. In spite of the deep loyalty and fervor of many of its sympathizers, there has never been an institutional determination of or organized efforts to preserve orthodoxy. Many of its most ardent adherents, says Andelson, do not hesitate to point out their disagreements with the master. This is of course, particularly true of academics, who are true to their nature more than to principles or personalities. Georgists do not subscribe to the notion that George's writings must be accepted as holy writ, but only that in the really crucial points where a "correct" viewpoint can be supported, George created or maintained that viewpoint. That some of his ideas are flawed does not change that basic point. He was a thinker of the first order; his economic methodology was sound and creative, so that his reform proposals retain lasting interest and relevance.

3. Those subject to such a tax would likely have an interest in concealing the idea from tax policymakers anxious to increase tax revenues. At the time this chapter was being drafted only the weak economy was suggesting that major tax increases should not be instituted across the board.

4. Ibid., p. 11.

References

Andelson, Robert V., 1994. *Henry George and the Reconstruction of Capitalism* (New York: Robert Schalkenbach Foundation; Great Barrington, Massachusetts: American Institute for Economic Research; and Saint Louis: Public Revenue Education Council). Available online at site of the School of Cooperative Individualism: http://www.cooperativeindividualism.org/andelson-robert_henry-george-reconstruction-of-capitalism.html, accessed on Jun. 30, 2010.

Andelson, Robert V., 2004. "Neo-Georgism," *The American Journal of Economics and Sociology,* Vol. 63, No. 2, pp. 543–69.

Arnott, Richard, 1979. "Optimal City Size in a Spatial Economy," *Journal of Urban Economics,* Vol. 6, No. 1, pp. 65–89.

Arnott, Richard, 2004. "Does the Henry George Theorem Provide a Practical Guide to Optimal City Size?" *The American Journal of Economics and Sociology,* Vol. 63, No. 5, pp. 1057–90.

Backhaus, Juergen G., 1997. *Land Value Taxation in Germany: Theoretical and Historical Issues.* Essay prepared for a Compendium on Land Value Taxation Around the World to be published on the occasion of the 100th anniversary of the death of Henry George. Available online at: http://landtax.co.il, accessed on Aug. 26, 1997.

Backhaus, Juergen G., 2004. "Increasing the Role of Environmental Taxes and Charges as a Policy Instrument in Developing Countries," *The American Journal of Economics and Sociology,* Vol. 63, No. 5, pp. 1097–130.

Barro, Robert J., 2009. "Government Spending Is No Free Lunch," *The Wall Street Journal,* Jan. 22.

Batt, William H., 2011. These views of Dr. Batt were shared with the author in an e-mail on Feb. 28, 2011.

Baumol, William J., 2004. "On Entrepreneurship, Growth and Rent-Seeking: Henry George Updated," *American Economist,* Vol. 48, No. 1, pp. 9–16.

Blaug, Mark, 1978. *Economic Theory in Retrospect,* 3rd Edition (London: Cambridge University Press).

Borcherding, Thomas E., Patricia Dillon and Thomas D. Willett, 1998. "Henry George: Precursor to Public Choice Analysis—Economist," *The American Journal of Economics and Sociology,* Vol. 57, No. 2, pp. 173–82.

Bowman, John H. and Michael E. Bell, 2008. "Distributional Consequences of Converting the Property Tax to a Land Value Tax: Replication and Extension of England and Zhao Authors," *National Tax Journal,* Vol. 61, No. 4, pp. 593–607.

Brown, H. James, 1997a. "Henry George's Contributions to Contemporary Studies of Land Use and Taxation," in H. James Brown, ed., *Land Use & Taxation: Applying the Insights of Henry George* (Cambridge, MA.: Lincoln Institute of Land Policy).

Brown, H. James and Martin O. Smolka, 1997b. "Capturing Public Value from Public Investment," in H. James Brown, ed., *Land Use & Taxation: Applying the Insights of Henry George* (Cambridge, MA.: Lincoln Institute of Land Policy), pp. 17–32.

Bryson, Phillip J., 2010. *The Economics of Centralism and Local Autonomy: Fiscal Decentralization in the Czech and Slovak Republics* (New York: Palgrave Macmillan).

DeNigris, Bob, 2007. *Henry George and the Single Tax* (Arden, Delaware: The Arden Georgist Gild). Available online at: http://www.henrygeorge.org/denigris.htm, accessed on Apr. 7, 2011.

Douglas, Roy, 1999. "The Rise of the British Land-Taxing Movement: How It All Began," in Kenneth C. Wenzer, ed., *Land-Value Taxation: The Equitable and Efficient Source of Public Finance* (New York: M. E. Sharpe), pp. 152–65.

Dwyer, Terence M., 1982. "Henry George's Thought in Relation to Modern Economics," *The American Journal of Economics and Sociology,* Vol. 41, No. 4, pp. 363–73.

England, Richard W. and Min Qiang Zhao, 2005. "Assessing the Distributive Impact of a Revenue–Neutral Shift from a Uniform Property Tax to a Two-Rate Property Tax with a Uniform Credit," *National Tax Journal*, Vol. 58, No. 2, pp. 247–60.

Foldvary, Fred E., 1999. "The Ethics of Rent," in Kenneth C. Wenzer, ed., *Land-Value Taxation: The Equitable and Efficient Source of Public Finance* (New York: M. E. Sharpe), pp. 184–204.

Friedman, Milton, 1962. *Capitalism and Freedom* (Chicago, IL: University of Chicago Press).

Gaffney, Mason, 1997. *Henry George 100 Years Later: The Great Reconciler.* Available online at: www.masongaffney.org/. . . /Henry_George_100_Years_Later.pdf, accessed on Nov. 17, 2010.

Gaffney, Mason, 1999. "Tax Reform to Release Land," in Kenneth C. Wenzer, ed., *Land-Value Taxation: The Equitable and Efficient Source of Public Finance* (New York: M. E. Sharpe), pp. 58–99.

Gaffney, Mason, 2001. "The Role of Ground Rent in Urban Decay and Revival: How to Revitalize a Failing City – Public Policy Implications," *The American Journal of Economics and Sociology*, Vol. 60, No. 5, pp. 55–84.

Gaffney, Mason and Fred Harrison, 1994. *The Corruption of Economics* (London: Shepheard-Walwyn Ltd.). Available online version is at: http://homepage.ntlworld.com/janusg/coe/!index.htm, accessed on Jul. 29, 2010.

Gehlhar, Mark, 1999. *Incorporating Transportation Costs into International Trade Models: Theory and Application* (Washington, D.C.: Economic Research Service, USDA).

George, Henry, 1879. *Progress and Poverty: An Inquiry into the Cause of Industrial Depressions and of Increase of Want with Increase of Wealth . . . The Remedy* (San Francisco: D. Appleton & Company). The version cited here was republished on CD, 2001 (Boston, MA: Lincoln Institute of Land Policy).

George, Henry, 1883. *Social Problems* (Boston, MA: Lincoln Institute of Land Policy, Republished from the original appearance in New York: Doubleday and McClure Company).

George, Henry, 1886. *Protection or Free Trade: An Examination of the Tariff Question, with Especial Regard to the Interests of Labor.* The Legacy and Works of Henry George in CD Format, 2001 (Boston, MA: Lincoln Institute of Land Policy).

George, Henry, 1892. *A Perplexed Philosopher, Being an Examination of Mr. Herbert Spencer's Various Utterances on the Land Question, with Some Incidental Reference to His Synthetic Philosophy.* The Legacy and Works of Henry George in CD Format, 2001 (Boston, MA: Lincoln Institute of Land Policy).

George, Henry, 1894. *The Condition of Labor: An Open Letter to Pope Leo XIII* (New York: Sterling Publishing Co.).

George, Henry, 1898. *The Science of Political Economy, A Reconstruction of Its Principles in Clear and Systematic Form.* The Legacy and Works of Henry George in CD Format, 2001 (Boston, MA: Lincoln Institute of Land Policy).

George, Henry, 1902. *Our Land and Land Policy: Speeches, Lectures, and Miscellaneous Writings* (Boston, MA: Lincoln Institute of Land Policy, Republished from the original appearance in New York: Doubleday and McClure Company).

George, Henry, Jr., 1900. *The Life of Henry George* (Honolulu, Hawaii: University Press of the Pacific, 2004, reprinted from the 1900 edition).

Gresser, Edward, 2002. "Toughest on the Poor: America's Flawed Tariff System," *Foreign Affairs,* Nov./Dec. 2002. Available online at: http://www.ppionline.org/ppi_ci.cfm?knlgAreaID= 108&subsecID=900010&contentID=250828, accessed on Aug. 3, 2010.

Harrison, Fred, 2003. "Longe and Wrightson: Conservative Critics of George's Wage Theory," *The American Journal of Economics and Sociology,* Vol. 62, No. 5, pp. 83–115.

Heavey, Jerome F., 2003. "Comments on Warren Samuels's 'why the Georgist movement has not succeeded,'" *The American Journal of Economics and Sociology,* Vol. 62, No. 3, pp. 593–99.

Hebert, Robert F., 2003. "Marshall: A Professional Economist Guards the Purity of His Discipline – Part II: Nineteenth-century British and Continental Critics," *The American Journal of Economics and Sociology,* Nov., pp. 61–82.

Holcombe, Randall G., 2004. "Echoes of Henry George in Modern Analysis," *The American Journal of Economics and Sociology,* Vol. 63, No. 5, pp. 1031–138.

Hummels, David, 1999. *Have International Transportation Costs Declined?* University of Chicago, Jul. 1999. Available online at: http://ntl.bts.gov/lib/24000/24400/24443/hummels.pdf, accessed on Aug. 3, 2010.

Irwin, Douglas A., 2006a. *Antebellum Tariff Politics: Coalition Formation and Shifting Regional Interests,* NBER Working Paper No. W12161.

Irwin, Douglas A., 2006b. *Tariff Incidence in America's Gilded Age,* NBER Working Paper No. W12162. Available online at SSRN: http://ssrn.com/abstract=896470, accessed on March 30, 2011.

Johnson, Harry G., 1954. "Optimum Tariffs and Retaliation," *Review of Economic Studies,* Vol. 21, No. 2, pp. 142–53.

Krueger, Anne O., 1974. "The Political Economy of the Rent Seeking Society," *American Economic Review,* Vol. 64, No. 3, pp. 291–303.

Lewis, Stephen R. (ed.), 1985. *Henry George and Contemporary Economic Development* (Williamstown, MA: Williams College).

List, Friedrich, 1845. "Gutachten über die wirtschaftliche Reform des Königsreichs Ungarn."

Marshall, Alfred, 1893. "On Rent," *Economic Journal,* Vol. 3, No. 9, Mar., pp. 74–90.

Marshall, Alfred, 1920. *Principles of Economics,* 9th Edition (Variorum), 1961 (London: Palgrave Macmillan).

Martin, Thomas L., 2001. "Protection or Free Trade: An Analysis of the Ideas of Henry George on International Commerce and Wages," *The American Journal of Economics and Sociology,* Vol. 60, No. 5, Nov., pp. 119–36.

Martinez-Vazquez, Jorge and Mark Rider, 2008. "The Assignment of the Property Tax: Should Developing Countries Follow the Conventional Wisdom?" "What Role for Property Taxes?" Conference: Andrew Young School of Policy Studies, International Studies Program, Georgia State University and The Lincoln Institute of Land Policy, Apr. 27–29, 2008. Available online at: http://aysps.gsu.edu, accessed on Oct. 29, 2010.

Milgrom, Paul R. and Robert J. Weber, 1982. "A Theory of Auctions and Competitive Bidding," *Econometrica,* Vol. 50, No. 5, pp. 1089–122.

Mill, John Stuart, 1848. *Principles of Political Economy with some of their Applications to Social Philosophy* (London: Longmans, Green and Co.).

Moss, Lawrence S., 2001. "Why the Preaching Must Never Stop: Henry George's and Paul Krugman's Respective Contributions to the Free Trade Debate," *The American Journal of Economics and Sociology,* Vol. 60, No. 5, pp. 137–64.

Pasinetti, Luigi L. and Roberto Scazzieri, 1987. "Capital Theory: Paradoxes," in John Eatwell, Murray Milgate and Peter Newman, eds., *The New Palgrave: A Dictionary of Economics, Vol. I.* (Houndmills: Palgrave Macmillan), pp. 363–68.

Plassmann, Florenz and T. Nicolaus Tideman, 2003. *A Framework for Assessing the Value of Downtown Land* (Virginia Polytechnic Institute and State University, Department of Economics Working Papers, number e07-5). Available online at: http://www2.binghamton.edu/economics/wp03/WP0306.pdf, accessed Apr. 1, 2011.

Pollard, Harry, 1979. "The Free Market of Henry George," The School of Comparative Individualism. Available online at: http://www.cooperativeindividualism.org/pollard-harry_henry-george-and-free-markets.html, accessed on Jun. 29, 2010.

Robinson, Joan, 1956. *Accumulation of Capital* (London: Palgrave Macmillan), pp. 109–10.

Samuelson, Paul A., 1994. "The Classical Classical Fallacy," *Journal of Economic Literature,* Vol. 32, No. 2, Jun., pp. 620–39.

Schumpeter, Joseph, 1954. *The History of Economic Analysis* (Oxford, England: Oxford University Press).

Schumpeter, Joseph A., 1954. *The History of Economic Analysis* (published posthumously), Elisabeth Boody Schumpeter, ed. (London: Allen & Unwin Ltd.).

Solow, Robert M., 1997. "How to Treat Intellectual Ancestors," in H. James Brown, ed., *Land Use & Taxation: Applying the Insights of Henry George* (Cambridge, MA: Lincoln Institute of Land Policy), pp. 7–16.

Sraffa, Piero, 1960. *Production of Commodities by Means of Commodities* (Cambridge: Cambridge University Press).

Stabile, Donald R., 1995. "Henry George's Influence on John Bates Clark: The Concept of Rent Was Pivotal to Equating Wages with the Marginal Product of Labor," *The American Journal of Economics and Sociology,* Vol. 54, No. 3, pp. 373–82.

Stiglitz, Joseph, 2003. "Interview with Christopher Williams," *Geophilos,* Spring, 2003. Available online at: http://www.wealthandwant.com/docs/Stiglitz_Oct02_interview.htm, accessed on Jul. 27, 2010.

Sullivan, Mark A., 2003. "Why the Georgist Movement Has Not Succeeded: A Personal Response to the Question Raised by Warren J. Samuels," *The American Journal of Economics and Sociology,* Vol. 62, No. 3, pp. 607–23.

Suranavic, Steven M., 2010. "The Stolper-Samuelson Theorem: Mathematical Derivation," published online by Creative Commons, *International Trade Theory and Policy.* Available online at: http://internationalecon.com/Trade/Tch115/T115-2.php, accessed on Aug. 3, 2010.

Tideman, Nicolaus, 2004. "George on Land Speculation and the Winner's Curse," *The American Journal of Economics and Sociology,* Vol. 63, No. 5, pp. 1091–95.

Tiebout, Charles M., 1956. "A Pure Theory of Local Expenditures," *The Journal of Political Economy,* Vol. 64, No. 5, pp. 416–24.

Tullock, Gordon, 1967. "The General Irrelevance of the General Impossibility Theorem," *Quarterly Journal of Economics,* Vol. 81, No. 5, pp. 256–70.

Vickrey, William, 1977. "The City as a Firm," in M. Feldstein and R. Inman, eds., *The Economics of Public Services* (London: Palgrave Macmillan), pp. 334–43.

Vickrey, William, 1999. "Henry George, Economies of Scale, and Land Taxation," in Kenneth C. Wenzer, ed., *Land-Value Taxation: The Equitable and Efficient Source of Public Finance* (New York: M.E. Sharpe), pp. 24–36.

Vickrey, William S., 2001. "Site Value Taxes and the Optimal Pricing of Public Services," *The American Journal of Economics and Sociology,* Vol. 60, No. 5, pp. 85–96.

Walker, Francis A., 1876. *The Wages Question: A Treatise on Wages and the Wages Class* (London: Palgrave Macmillan and Co.).

Walker, Francis A., 1879. "Money in Its relation to Trade and Industry," *New Englander and Yale Review,* Vol. 38, No. 153, Nov., p. 847.

Wasserman, Louis, 2003. "The Essential Henry George – Part I: Prolegomena," *The American Journal of Economics and Sociology,* Vol. 62, No. 5, pp. 23–43.

Whitaker, John J., 1997. "Enemies or Allies? Henry George and Francis Amasa Walker One Century Later," *Journal of Economic Literature,* Vol. 35, No. 4, Dec., pp. 1891–915.

Youngman, Joan and Jane Malme (eds.), 2001. The Development of Property Taxation in Economies in Transition: Case Studies from Central and Eastern Europe (Washington, D.C.: The World Bank).

Index